Trip to Vietra

WOMEN ON THE MOVE

WOMEN ON THE MOVE
HANOI'S MIGRANT ROVING STREET VENDORS

Rolf Jensen
Donald M. Peppard Jr.
Vũ Thị Minh Thắng

Women's Publishing House
Vietnam

Published in Vietnam by
Women's Publishing House - Vietnam
39 Hang Chuoi Street
Hanoi

ISBN: 978-604-56-1834-9

This publication was made possible, in part, with a grant from the
International School of Vietnam National University - Hanoi.

To the many women who leave their homes and families to work in Hanoi as roving street vendors, in the hope that no one who reads this book will ever again pass by one without a better understanding of the difficult and complicated life she leads.

TABLE OF CONTENTS

LIST OF TABLES

LIST OF TEXT BOXES

ACKNOWLEGEMENTS

This book has grown out of more than a decade's work with Hanoi's migrant roving street vendors. Little did we know in 1999, when we, Jensen and Peppard, first became interested in this group of women, that our curiosity about them would cause us to devote the next 13 years to this project. What began as a Connecticut College faculty-student research project in 2000, quickly evolved into an annual effort to modify and extend our original survey work. As the project progressed, we were lucky to be able to bring in Vũ to enable us to delve more deeply into the nature of street vendors' rural and urban lives, some of it very personal, and into how the rapidly changing nature of Vietnam's economy was affecting them and their families.

The project has involved many of our students from Connecticut College. We have benefitted immensely from the work they have done while interviewing hundreds of roving street vendors in the streets of Hanoi each year. Their work was made possible by students from several universities in Hanoi who worked as translators. We do not have enough space to list the names of all of the students who worked with us over the years, but we owe them a deep debt of gratitude for their careful efforts on our behalf.

Our work on this book has brought us into contact with colleagues throughout the Vietnamese university system, and it also expanded to include a set of three documentary films on the lives and stories of street vendors that Jensen produced in collaboration with the Vietnamese Women's Museum in Hanoi. We would especially like to thank Đỗ Thị Hương Thảo of the Faculty of History, University of Social Sciences and

Humanities at Vietnam National University – Hanoi and Phạm Thị Mỹ Dung of the Faculty of Economics and Rural Development at Hanoi Agricultural University. We also thank the faculty, both past and current, of the Economics University at Vietnam National University – Hanoi and the staff, past and current, of the Vietnamese Women's Museum.

We are grateful to Connecticut College for the many opportunities it gave Jensen and Peppard to be in Vietnam in order to pursue this research, and we appreciate funding assistance from the R. Francis Johnson Fund that helped support it. We are equally grateful to the Faculty of Political Science, University of Social Sciences and Humanities at Vietnam National University – Hanoi for providing release time that allowed Vũ to conduct research for the book. We thank Vũ Ngọc Tú, vice-Rector, and Đinh Đức Long, Director of Administrative Affairs, of the International School of Vietnam National University – Hanoi for many years of friendship as well as logistical support. We also thank Nguyễn Trọng Do, Rector of the International School of Vietnam National University – Hanoi.

Finally, we thank our families for the encouragement they have given us over the many years we have been working on this book.

CHAPTER 1

INTRODUCTION

As any visitor to Hanoi knows, one of the most impressive things about the capital city of Vietnam[1] is how busy its streets and nearby spaces are. Motorbikes compete with cars and buses for street space, and traffic congestion and noise seem overwhelming at times. The city is densely populated, with an average density of about 2000 persons per square kilometer that is up to 10 times higher in the densest district.[2] The high population density arises because most people live in multi-story houses on very small plots of land, without yards or gardens, or in large apartment buildings. This density means that there are few public places other than sidewalks and parks for children to play and for adults to socialize. Many families use the ground floors of residential buildings for commercial uses, as a source of income, and live on the upper floors. Because there is little room for parking on the streets, sidewalks become parking spaces for motorbikes and cars as their drivers patronize stores and go to their workplaces.

In addition to their uses as places to play, socialize, and providing access to retail shops that open onto them, sidewalks are also places for street vendors to set up and sell. A huge variety of goods and services are sold from stands and spaces on sidewalks. It is common to find on the sidewalks people selling all manner of goods and services: uncooked and prepared food, spillover seating for restaurants, shoe shines, flowers, motorbike and bicycle repairs, and more. When customers park on the sidewalk to patronize the vendors and shops, and while children play and adults supervise their children's play, it often becomes difficult for pedestrians to walk on sidewalks, so many move into the streets. All this activity sometimes blurs the boundary between street and sidewalk.[3]

Most commercial uses of the sidewalks make up an important part of what is known as the urban informal sector of Vietnam's economy.[4] Among the many people who participate in this sector are rural people who migrate to Hanoi for days, weeks, or months at a time. We have chosen to focus this book on one group of these circular migrants, women who walk around the city carrying the goods they sell in baskets that hang from a bamboo pole across their shoulders. These women live two lives, one in the countryside as members of farming families and another in Hanoi where they work in the informal sector as roving street vendors. They work in all parts of the city, often laboring under poles that look as though they might break from the weight they support and wearing conical hats that clearly mark them as rural people. (Most Hanoi residents rarely, if ever, wear this type of hat that ironically has become a symbol of Vietnam.)

Many Hanoians want the city to appear more modern and orderly and have supported attempts to reduce some uses of the sidewalks by making many of them off-limits to the selling activities of street vendors. Further, rapidly rising urban incomes make the selling activities of many street vendors less and less attractive to urbanites. Thus, while the informal sector continues to be easy to enter for people lacking skills and education, it is also a sector in which it is becoming more difficult to operate. This means that roving street vendors, or basket ladies as they are often called,[5] and many others who depend on this sector to supplement rural incomes are in a squeeze that threatens their ability to remain farmers.

For many years, it has been clear both to rural people themselves and to outside researchers that incomes from farming are insufficient and that a large number of rural families simply cannot survive on agriculture alone.[6] However, most rural people do not want to uproot their families in order to move to a city. That leaves as one option what the families of roving street vendors have chosen to do: send a member of the family to a city to earn that essential extra income.

In order to better understand the complicated lives of basket ladies, therefore, it is necessary to look at both the rural and urban components of those lives and at how the two interact. These women are very strongly tied not only to their families who remain in the countryside but also to their villages through customs and traditions. Even while they live and work in Hanoi, those ties loom large in their lives. They tend to live in rooming houses with other women from their villages or communes, all the while missing their children and families back home. In this book, we present a close look at the rural and urban lives of roving street vendors. We also look at the multitude of reasons that lead these families to the decision for the wife rather than her husband to migrate. To illustrate in a more personalized way the many generalizations we make about migrant street vendor lives, we use text boxes throughout the book to give examples from the lives of individual basket ladies.

The roving street vendors who are the focus of this book also cast light on a larger group of rural dwellers who try to retain their rural roots and lives by earning urban incomes. First, not all roving street vendors in Hanoi are circular migrants, but the vast majority of them are rural.[7] Largely because of their proximity to the city of Hanoi, some basket ladies are able to come into town on a daily basis and return to their villages each night. Second, basket ladies are only one group among many who migrate to work in Hanoi's informal sector. By focusing on the lives of circular migrant street vendors, therefore, we illuminate the lives of many more rural families in Vietnam. In important ways, many of those other rural families have much in common with the families of roving street vendors: inadequate land holdings, a precarious existence near the poverty line, and a complex web of village family and social networks.

Vietnam's Transition Economy[8]

When what the Vietnamese call the "American War" ended in 1975, the government was faced with at least two daunting tasks: how to make a unified country from the two pieces into which it had been split in 1954, and how to operate a peacetime economy in the whole country for the first time since the 1930s. The former task was made more difficult because of the very different institutions and customs that had

3

grown up in the two regions, north and south, during the time of partition. The south had been dominated by American money and capitalist markets, while the north had modeled itself on the central planning and advice of the Soviet Union. In the latter case, wartime dedication to the central goal of victory and the important support of outside donors gave way after 1975 to the more amorphous goals of feeding the population and providing consumer and industrial goods in the absence of large gifts of outside aid.[9]

A variety of problems beset the economy during the period between 1975 and 1985. Among the more serious of these problems were shortages in food and manufactured goods that led to both very high inflation rates and rising rates of hunger. Finally, in 1986, the government began a series of fundamental reforms called "*Doi Moi*" (renovation). There is almost total agreement among observers of the recent political, social, and economic history of Vietnam that these reforms were remarkably successful. The transition from an economy modeled on the Soviet system to a largely market-driven economy with far less government involvement in everyday matters has led to plummeting poverty rates as a result of very rapid economic growth. In addition, Vietnam has avoided most of the wrenching and traumatic changes experienced in some other countries making similar transitions.[10]

The transition in Vietnam that started in 1986 accelerated in the early 1990s. Among the most important of the reforms was to free farmers from collective labor and allocation of their output to produce for whatever uses they saw fit. Land use rights now give farmers incentives to improve their land and produce crops that may earn more than the traditional rice crop. However, rice remains the most important crop, and the increase in its production that resulted from the land reforms is one of the most important achievements of *Doi Moi*. The extent of the changes and the consequence of releasing the energy of farmers are such that Vietnam went from widespread food shortages in the mid-1980s to being a food exporter by the early 1990s.

In addition, individuals were allowed to operate businesses and participate in market activities that had previously been prohibited. In their nuanced explanations of Vietnam's success after the reforms, Van Arkadie and Mallon stress that the reforms began a process that continues to this day, the long-run success of which has to be explained by factors other than the reforms themselves: "A combination of improved incentives, increased competition, and reductions in barriers to the adoption of existing knowledge are crucial to explaining the rapid improvements in economic performance over the last 20 years."[11]

Vietnam continues to make the transition to what it calls a "socialist-oriented market economy." Macroeconomic growth has been impressive: from 1997 through 2010, GDP growth averaged about 7 percent per year.[12] While the country remains a largely rural society (approximately 70 percent of the population was rural in 2010[13]), it is rapidly urbanizing. As it is growing and urbanizing, Vietnam's economy is also rapidly industrializing, and its service sector is also growing. From 1995 to 2005, industrial output increased at a rate of 10 percent per year, and services increased 5.7 percent per year.[14] Finally, Vietnam joined the World Trade Organization (WTO) in January, 2007.

Part of the reason for the success in Vietnam is the political stability conferred by the one-party state. While much else has changed dramatically since 1986, the Communist Party continues to dominate political decision-making in Vietnam. Political stability provided a context in which the many other changes that began to occur in 1986 could proceed smoothly. However, even though the political organization has remained largely unchanged, the role of the state is quite different from what it once was.[15] Now, market forces take the place of much of the central planning that had been attempted between 1975 (earlier in the north) and 1985.

The changes that occurred after *Doi Moi* were dramatic in other respects as well. An important consequence of the *Doi Moi* reforms was that responsibility for the economic well-being of the family was transferred from the state to the family itself. In addition to being responsible for meeting their own food needs, families increasingly turned to the market in order to meet their non-food needs. The movement toward an economy in which markets play an ever-larger role meant that people were free to seek employment, including self-employment, in activities that had previously been restricted and/or illegal. These included the sale of goods and services directly to consumers, often in the informal sector. For example, Koh notes at least two causes of increased sidewalk vending activities in Hanoi. The first was "the drastic reduction of the state sector, which had provided most, if not all, the employment in Vietnam," and the second was that after 1988, farmers were able to sell their output directly to the market.[16] Both former state employees and former collective farmers were able to join what had been up to that point a small part of Vietnam's economy—the informal, non-state sector. They joined the informal sector then for reasons that people continue to join it now: too few other employment opportunities for people without skills or much education.

The burden on women who migrate to work in the urban informal sector in order to maintain the economic well-being of their families has increased dramatically. This falls on top of other burdens that the post-*Doi Moi* focus on the family has placed on them. Werner, for example, notes the increased burdens that family and ceremonial obligations have placed on women.[17] An important theme that we develop in this book is how, in the case of migrant street vendors, some of the burdens placed on women require that they be at home while others require that they be in Hanoi. How they meet these often-conflicting burdens is part of what makes their lives so interesting and also so difficult.

Part of the transition that is going on in Vietnam is also a transition from traditional ways of doing things to more modern methods. For example, urban dwellers go out to eat more than they did, and they are increasingly buying food for home consumption differently from the old ways. The transition from traditional to modern, however, means the coexistence, at least for now, of two food distribution systems. Modern supermarkets and small shops are proliferating in the formal food distribution network, and street vendors and sidewalk stalls are firmly rooted in the informal food distribution network. The neighborhood market, perhaps the most important place to buy food, has both formal and informal aspects. For example, these markets are subject to some regulation by the authorities, but they are made up of self-employed vendors or very small stalls that employ one or two people.

Roving street vendors in Hanoi, consequently, are at the intersection of colliding forces in Vietnam: between traditional mores, modes of behavior, and occupations on one side and trends that stress efficiency and the importance of modernity on the other. These vendors are part of a pattern of rising inequality between rich and poor, between urban and rural, and between educated and uneducated. Basket ladies find themselves caught between government attempts to reduce or eliminate the old from a city striving to be modern and a recognition that rural people cannot live on agricultural incomes alone. These opposing forces push and pull the people in our study in often sad ways, such as when debt threatens to make poverty perpetual, or when mothers are pushed by financial reasons to leave their children and families for long periods of time. However, at this time, the ability of roving street vendors to leave their villages and supplement agricultural income is the only way that they and their families are able to maintain both rural residences and rural lifestyles.

We believe the women in this book also represent an example of the success of Vietnam's reforms: virtually all of the women with whom we and our students have spoken since 2000 began their work as roving street sellers after the advent of *Doi Moi*. Therefore, they have taken advantage of the ability of families to control their economic lives and reap the benefits that private sales can confer. They represent a classic example of what happens when an occupation can be entered easily and cheaply: many people who see the opportunity to earn greater incomes in another job enter that job when it is convenient or, in the case of most of the women we have met, when it is necessary to do so. In order to do this urban job, they need to leave behind, for varying periods of time, their families and their rural homes. Thus, these women are part of a much larger group of migrants, people who leave their homes to work and sometimes to live in different places.

The future of many activities that occur in Hanoi's urban informal sector will depend in part on how quickly certain changes take place. It is likely that in the future the actions of both city officials and erstwhile customers of basket ladies will have important effects. The intense use of the sidewalks and streets that we noted earlier, with modern and traditional activities taking place at the same time, makes Hanoi a city in which sidewalk congestion adds to street congestion to generate many traffic accidents. In 2003, city officials noted the existence of "tens of thousands of street vendors and pavement [sidewalk]-based family businesses, which are considered major contributors to Ha Noi's already chaotic traffic..."[18] Consequently, city officials have periodically tried to control commercial uses of the sidewalks.[19] These attempts continue to the present and are part of the threats to which informal sector, sidewalk-using vendors are increasingly subject. In Chapter 4 of this book, we discuss the nature of the police threat to basket lady livelihoods, and we analyze how changing customer behavior and attitudes are also affecting the ability of roving street vendors to earn income in Hanoi.

Much more needs to be known about women's circular migration. We believe this book contributes to that knowledge by looking at the many aspects of rural life that give rise to the need to migrate, by explaining the decision in the case of roving street vendors for the wife and not her husband to be the one who migrates, by describing how basket ladies live and work while they are in Hanoi, and by showing how important that work is in helping families retain their rural identities.

Methodology

In order to present the lives of roving street vendors and to tell their stories, we have taken two approaches to gathering information. First, our students, aided by Vietnamese translators, have conducted surveys with more than 2000 vendors since the year 2000: 379 in 2000, 431 in 2001, 286 in 2003, and more than 900 from 2006 to 2012. In the 2000, 2001, and 2003 surveys we selected interview subjects at random and all over the city. Thus, we surveyed all types of roving street vendors, including daily migrants and Hanoi residents along with circular migrants. In 2006, however, we purposely chose an unrepresentative group—only circular migrants—so that we could focus on patterns of migration and the division of child-care responsibilities within the families of circular migrants. In 2007, 2008 and 2010, we once again surveyed only circular migrants who worked in five central districts of Hanoi in order to learn more about their living arrangements while working in the city and about the division of household responsibilities among family members. In 2009 and 2010, we learned about the details of the performance of household tasks both when the street vendor was in Hanoi and when she was home.

To put the street vending job into context, we conducted other types of surveys as well: in 2001, we designed and implemented with the help of Vietnamese students a survey of the customers of basket ladies in order to determine, among other things, the occupations of their typical customers. In 2004, we worked with colleagues from the Economics faculty of Vietnam National University—Hanoi to interview more than 200 people buying food from all types of vendors, from street vendors to supermarkets. At that time we learned a great deal about customer attitudes toward buying food in all venues.[20] Finally, in 2012 our students conducted another survey of food-buying customers in order to gain as current a view of their opinions as possible.

Our second approach to gathering the information used in this book is in-depth interviews. Beginning in 2003, we interviewed 30 other vendors in depth to learn their life stories in great detail. We then "followed" a subset of eight of these women and re-interviewed them several times over the next 5-6 years, giving us a sense of how rapid change in Vietnam has affected them and their families. The text boxes we use in the following chapters are drawn from these longer, more detailed and informative interviews.

The rapid and successful transformation of Vietnam's economy is imposing on rural dwellers a variety of stresses and strains, from the need to learn how to grow new crops to increasing agricultural productivity. In addition, it has long been the case that agricultural incomes have been insufficient for many rural families, some of whom have sought extra income in low-skilled urban work.

In the following chapters, we lay out what we have learned about the families and economic lives of roving street vendors. Based on what they have told us, we explain why basket ladies do this work, what often makes it so hard, how their families cope in their absence, and what we and they think are their prospects for the future.

In Chapter 2 we focus on various aspects of life in villages in and around the Red River Delta. These include family life, ceremonial traditions, education, housing, patterns of land distribution and agricultural production, animal husbandry, debt, and family living expenses. We show how many of these aspects of village life impose obligations of time on a street vendor that require her to be present in her village in order to perform them. However, these aspects also impose financial obligations that require her to be in Hanoi to earn money. Unwilling to give up their rural identities, circular migration becomes the way that street vendors try to meet these often conflicting sets of obligations.

Chapter 3 begins with a discussion of the importance of the incomes that street vendors earn in Hanoi, in light of different poverty thresholds and in terms of the national distribution of income and consumption. We use hypothetical examples to show the changes in living standards that would occur if their families were to gain or lose this income. Following that, we consider a series of questions concerning the decision to migrate. We look first at why women go to Hanoi to work as circular migrants instead of working closer to home. We also discuss why the woman and not her husband is the one to migrate, and we examine how issues of child bearing and child rearing affect the timing of the decision of a woman to go to Hanoi and the pattern of migration that she adopts. Finally, we look at how the decision of a woman to migrate affects gender roles within the family with respect to household chores, child rearing, and agricultural production. In order to make it easier for readers to choose whether to pursue in more detail some of the literature about migration, both theoretical and empirical for Vietnam, we place our survey of that literature in an appendix to the book.

Chapter 4 examines how women perform their jobs as roving street vendors in Hanoi's informal sector and the lives they live while they are in Hanoi. We begin with a description of how, even in Hanoi, women continue to be tied to and affected by village and family relationships.

The chapter includes a detailed description of the "business" of street vending: how they buy their goods and set prices; how they decide where to sell; how much money they make; and the risks they face while selling, including frequent and expensive confrontations with police. We also describe the often difficult conditions under which migrant street vendors live when they are in Hanoi.

In the conclusion, we discuss our most recent survey results and the implications of continued modernization and rapid change in Hanoi for the lives of street vendors. We also suggest a change in policy toward street vendors on the part of Vietnamese authorities and offer an explanation in support of our suggestion.

CHAPTER 2

VILLAGE LIFE

Village life is comprised in part of a complex set of social relations that help shape a roving street vendor's rural identity as well as her identity as a migrant female worker in the urban informal sector. This set of social relations, in turn, is associated with an equally complex set of beliefs and practices that mutually reinforce and are reinforced by those social relations. In this chapter, we analyze village life and many of the social relations, beliefs, and practices that help comprise it.

The notion of Vietnamese rural or village society itself can be misleading, especially if it is thought of as a homogenous entity even within different regions of the country. Most villages in Vietnam have their own important and in many ways unique histories, and these often cause significant differences in the ways that social relations, beliefs, and practices are constituted from one village to another. It would be wrong to attempt to analyze rural life anywhere in Vietnam without recognizing that such differences exist. Nonetheless, the insights into rural life contained in this chapter may be helpful in understanding the lives not only of migrant roving street vendors but of other female migrants in Vietnam as well.

We also do not pretend in this chapter to produce an exhaustive account of rural life in the provinces from which roving street vendors come. Instead, we intend a more narrowly focused study here. We will look how the social relations, beliefs, and practices help shape part of the general support network that is crucial to the survival of a roving street vendor and her family. We also look at how these relations, beliefs, and practices combine to produce what can often be a conflicting set of obligations on her and her family. On the one hand, these obligations include financial ones which require that a street vendor be in Hanoi in order to earn money to help her family meet them. On the other hand, they may also require that she be physically present in her village, even if it means leaving Hanoi in order to return. Together, these obligations figure prominently in how a roving street vendor allocates her time between Hanoi and her village.

Family Life

Historically, the family and a woman's place within it have played a pivotal role in Vietnamese society. That role has also changed over the course of the successive struggles for national independence and reunification and the subsequent struggles to build a national socialism first in opposition to and then in an embrace of at least some aspects of free-market capitalism. An important aspect of these struggles has resulted in an attempt to forge a national identity that is based in part on the principle of gender equality.[21] However, family culture remains strongly influenced by a Confucian tradition with which it has long been intertwined. In part because of this influence, roving street vendors, like most rural women, continue to see themselves largely in and through their relationships to men. In these relationships, furthermore, they are expected to assume a subordinate role. Although the government tried in the periods both before and after national reunification to eliminate many aspects of the Confucian tradition as remnants of a feudal past, even some of the more repressive aspects of that tradition, such as the principles of the "three obediences" and the "four virtues," have not entirely disappeared from the ways that some roving street vendors talk about themselves and their lives.

These principles teach that a woman will be dependent upon three men over the course of her lifetime and mandate specific types of behavior that she, first as a young girl and then as a woman, will be expected to play. The first of these men is her father, the second her husband, and the third, in the event that her husband dies before she does, her son. In each of these relationships, the man is considered to be the "pillar" of his own family, and the woman is integrated into that man's family as a subordinate member. She is taught at an early age that she will be expected to exhibit qualities that include being, "obedient," "respectful," "tender," "patient," "sacrificing," "modest," and "hard-working," all terms that roving street vendors continue to use today when talking about themselves and their families.[22]

In almost all cases, the gender roles that a woman is expected to play at various phases of her life conform to widely accepted village norms. In ways that are both taught and felt, she knows that any behavior on her part that deviates from these norms will subject her to public scrutiny and gossip. More importantly, it can bring shame on her entire

---

But not everyone wanted to drop out of school...

When Hoi was a young girl in her village in Ha Tay Province, she was part of a group of ten friends who decided at an early age that they all wanted to become teachers. However, only five of them passed the high school entrance exam. Hoi took the exam a second time but again did not pass it. Then, she decided to enroll in a high school equivalency program. Her father was very sick at the time, and although her parents encouraged her to drop out of school completely, they supported her decision. She went to class three days a week and took a job with the local embroidery cooperative on the other days. Half way through the 10th grade, however, the 1979 war with China broke out, and because Hoi was not enrolled in a regular high school, she was drafted into the army. She served in the army for three years, and then returned to work full-time in the embroidery cooperative until it was dissolved in 1983. She had gotten married shortly before this, and because she and her husband had no money and were hungry almost all of the time, she started coming to Hanoi to work as a roving street vendor. Had she been allowed to finish the equivalency program, she says she would have done her best to continue her plans to become a teacher.

The five friends who passed the exam all went to become teachers. Of the remaining four friends, one is in poor health and works only as a farmer. The other three, like Hoi, work as roving street vendors in Hanoi. Hoi stays in touch with all of the women but says that there is now a distance between those who became teachers and those who did not. She says that the teachers have an air of superiority about the different directions their lives have taken, and when she once joked about her two sons marrying two of their daughters, they told her that she would have make sure that they, at least, were able to finish high school.

---

family, violating one of the most sacred taboos of village culture. In the early period of *Doi Moi*, the integration of a woman into the modern market economy as a migrant roving street vendor did pose a significant challenge to the norms in many villages, but almost all street vendors say that it is now widely accepted for a woman to leave her home in order to work in Hanoi. Even so, each village has developed a new set of norms that govern the conditions under which this work is supposed to be performed.

With a median age of 35, most of today's roving street vendors were born before the start of the *Doi Moi* period, and their childhood family experiences were in some ways quite different from those of rural children today. Almost all went to school where they learned to read, write, and do simple arithmetic calculations, but most did not go beyond middle school. Many of them dropped out of school because all of their friends also decided to drop out, while others quit simply because they did not like it or because they did not feel smart enough to continue. These reasons, however, are almost always in addition to the overwhelming response that they dropped out of school because their families were too poor for them to go on. In some instances, this was because the local high school was too far away from their homes, and they would have needed a bicycle to get to school each day or their parents would have had to pay for them to live with another family closer to the school. In other cases, their parents might have been willing to send them to high school if they had really wanted to go, but they themselves felt this would have caused too much hardship for their families. Whatever the reasons, going on to high school was simply not an issue for almost all of today's roving street vendors.[23]

After leaving school, usually around the age of 14, some girls got jobs outside of agriculture in order to help their parents, but the majority of them stayed at home to help out with household chores, to look after their younger siblings, and to help with farm work. Part of the reason for this is that there were very few non-agricultural jobs to be had, except for girls who lived in or near craft villages or villages specializing in the production of processed foods such as tofu or rice noodles. It was only as they got older and a bit stronger that a few of them took on jobs as brick carriers at traditional brickmaking factories in or near their villages. Whatever they wound up doing, however, seems to have been motivated by the overwhelming sense of duty that most of them felt to help their parents in any ways they could after dropping out of school. In fact, very few of them say that their parents actually forced them to drop out of school. Instead, the idea of continuing their education beyond middle school was a luxury that none of them felt they could impose on their families.

Virtually all roving street vendors were born into rural farm families, and it was expected that they would continue to be farmers once they got married. This was typically at the age of 17 or 18, although in some cases it could be a year or two later. In the rare case where a woman had not gotten married by then, she either did not get married at all, or if she did, it would often be to an older man from another province who for one reason or another was looking to get married. Otherwise, the preferred age for a husband was a man who was a few years older, and he usually came from the same commune or from one that was nearby.

For the most part, street vendors are now free to choose their own husbands, and in the one case we did come across in which a woman's parents had arranged a marriage for her, if she had been opposed to the idea she would not have had to accept it.[24] The opinion of the family concerning a marriage partner, however, continues to be of paramount importance, and if the parents of either an

Loi's daughter, Ha, and her two young daughters live at home with Loi back in her village...
Ha had the children out of wedlock with a young man from the city of Hai Phong where she had gone to work after dropping out of school. The two of them had planned to get married, but the man's parents refused to consent to his marrying someone from the country, so the wedding never took place. In an attempt to save face and prevent gossip, Loi and her husband arranged a 'fake' wedding ceremony meal back in their village to which 120 people were invited. The young man agreed to attend and even brought a few distant relatives to act as the official representatives of the groom's family. Then, after her daughter returned to the village a short while later, Loi told people that the husband had become a drug addict and that Ha had left him.

intended bride or bridegroom do not give their consent to the marriage, it would be almost unheard of for the couple go ahead and get married. To do so would bring shame on the families involved and put intense social pressure on the couple itself.

Once married, most of a woman's responsibilities shift from her own family to that of her husband. Rural residence patterns are patrilocal, so she is expected to live with her husband as soon as the marriage takes place. The two of them usually live with the husband's parents and are considered to be members of their household. The husband's parents then decide when the couple is allowed to form an independent household of their own. This practice has often imposed harsh conditions on a newly married woman. As long as she is a member of her parents-in-law's household, they make most important decisions for her, including whether she is allowed to work at a job outside of agriculture and if so, whether she is allowed to migrate in order to find work. In terms of farming, it means that the woman and her husband do not have independent control over their own land, and the husband's parents manage the production as well as

Thuy got married in 1985 at the age of 17...
Her husband went into the army for two years immediately after they got married, and Thuy moved to her husband's village to live alone with his parents. From the time she quit school after 7th grade until she got married, Thuy worked for a kiln owner in the pottery village of Bat Trang. Her first job was to cut straw in the mornings and to sweep out the kiln in the afternoons. Later, she was taught how to apply stencil designs on small tea cups, and after that she learned how to glaze and started to paint designs on unbaked soup bowls. Thuy liked the idea of a job with a steady income and wanted to keep working there after she got married, but her parents-in-law made her quit so that she could work in their fields and help out around the house. Thuy believes that had she been able to keep the job in Bat Trang, she would have been able to become a skilled glazer, and she still thinks about what her life might have been like with a steady job and a regular flow of income. She compares this to her current job as a street vendor in Hanoi where she never knows how much money she will make from one day to the next, but she also acknowledges that she probably makes more money working in Hanoi at a job that offers her much more flexibility than the job she had to give up.

the distribution of rice and other crops. Similarly, household chores performed by the newly married woman are performed under the oversight of her mother-in-law.

After a woman and her husband form their own independent household, they often continue to live in the same house but no longer share meals or household and agricultural tasks. Still, it is generally expected that she will have to assume other obligations to her parents-in-law, especially as they get older. These include paying medical costs and can also include the obligation to either grow or buy enough food for the in-laws to eat. To an important extent, these obligations will depend on her husband's status within the family since the oldest son is expected to continue living in the same house as his parents when they get older and to assume primary responsibility for their care. However, other sons and their wives can be called upon to help out if the expenses become unmanageable, and very few street vendors are able entirely to escape helping with the care of the parents-in-law. The same holds true of a woman's obligations to other members of her husband's family if any of them run into financial difficulties and need money. The fact that she and her husband may themselves be in financial difficulty does not normally relieve them of these family obligations.

Ceremonial Life

Village social life is marked by a number of ceremonial rituals, social rites of passage, and other commemorative occasions. These rituals not only serve as a cohesive force to reinforce the street vendor's bonds within her own family, they also serve to reinforce her integration within the larger social network of friends, neighbors, and other people from her village. As a result, they often require a street vendor's presence in her village, and even in cases where they do not, they almost always impose a financial obligation on her family.

Lunar Holidays
Tet marks the beginning of the lunar new year, and the celebration of Tet is the most important ceremonial ritual of the year. Because it falls on the second new moon after the winter solstice, Tet is always in either January or February.[25] The Tet holiday period can last more than a month

and includes several important ceremonies. The first of these is the kitchen ceremony, which takes place on the 23rd day of the 12th lunar month, one week before Tet. On this day the three kitchen spirits are thought to visit the Celestial Emperor to report on the affairs of the family over the course of the previous year. Then, on the last day of the year, each family celebrates its ancestors with a meal consisting of fruit, meat, and poultry. This meal, and the ancestral offering prepared on the following day, Tet itself, represent the two most important meals of the year for the family. The first five days of Tet then involve a series of visits between relatives, friends, and neighbors during which they exchange wishes for the new year. The 15th day of the first lunar month is another ceremonial occasion and often coincides with the meal marking the official end of Tet. The actual day of this last meal, however, varies according to such factors as family tradition, the socio-economic status of the family, and superstition, and it can take place anytime during the first lunar month.

Celebrating Tet means that families often must be prepared to spend large sums of money. The kitchen ceremony involves an offering of either live or paper fish, which have to be bought and which are believed to be necessary in order to transport the kitchen spirits to the heavens so that they can make their report on the family. Family and village tradition may also dictate that parents buy new clothes for their children to wear for the holidays. The ceremonial meals during this period are the among the most festive and expensive of the year. In the days leading up to Tet relatives, neighbors, and friends exchange gifts of fruit, candy, biscuits, tea, and alcohol. Then, on Tet and on the days that follow, families give gifts of cash as they make their rounds of visits to friends and relatives.

A roving street vendor must be at home with her family for Tet. More than a simple obligation, this is a time of year that street vendors enjoy and genuinely want to be back in their villages to spend time with their children and their families. One dilemma that they face is that the days leading up to Tet are marked by a buying frenzy on the part of Hanoi residents as they too prepare for the holidays. Most street vendors are reluctant to go home during this period and choose instead to remain in Hanoi for as long as possible. For many of them, this means that they do not go home for the day of the kitchen ceremony and instead prolong their stays in Hanoi well into the last week of the lunar year. Some even remain in Hanoi for the entire week before returning home for the ceremonial meal on the eve of Tet. They say that this is something that is noticed by others back at home but that the amount of money they can earn is enough to risk public scrutiny and gossip.

Whenever it is that they return home, few street vendors would even think about coming back to Hanoi during the first five days of the lunar new year. Indeed, most of them would prefer to remain at home for as long as possible, and they often stay at least until after the celebration of the first full moon of the year on the 15th day. Others stay at home for the entire month, taking advantage of the time to begin working on their rice fields and simply to rest. Still, many street vendors do find that they must come back to Hanoi at some point during the first lunar month, even if it is only for a few days, in order to keep up the family cash flow.[26]

There are a number of other lunar holidays, which, while not nearly as important as Tet, nonetheless play an important role in the lives of roving street vendors. Among these are the 3rd day of the 3rd lunar month, the 5th day of the 5th lunar month, and the 15th days of the 7th and 8th lunar months. The 3rd day of the 3rd lunar month is sometimes known as the "floating cake" holiday in which a family's ancestors are celebrated with an offering of small rice flour cakes stuffed with either a sugared plum or with green bean paste. The holiday also involves visits to ancestral gravesites so that family members can clean up around the site. The 5th day of the 5th lunar month is a mid-year festival that is rooted in Vietnamese folklore and involves the preparation of a fermented sticky rice drink intended to kill off any parasites that a person might have. The 15th day of the 7th lunar month celebrates the wandering souls of people throughout the nation who died without leaving behind any family members who could give them a proper burial. The 15th day of the following month is an autumn celebration that has become perhaps best known as a holiday for children because of all of the colorful cakes, candies, and toys that they expect to be given.[27]

21

It is common for street vendors to return home for several if not all of these celebrations, even if only for a day or two. While they represent important holidays in terms of Vietnamese culture, their importance in terms of the lives of roving street vendors goes beyond any ritual or spiritual significance they may have. Indeed, not all street vendors are fully aware of the historical and cultural reasons for all of these ceremonial holidays. Instead, for many if not most roving street vendors, they represent important benchmarks around which they can organize their time. The months following Tet, especially the 2nd through the 5th months and then again after the second rice crop is planted in the 6th lunar month, tend to be the months in which street vendors spend relatively long periods of time working in Hanoi. The demands for them to be at home during these months are often not as great as in other months, and it is hard for many of them to justify returning home instead of remaining in the city to make money. At the same time, the weather gets progressively hotter during these months, and many of them complain about the emotional and physical strain of the job as the heat and humidity rise and as the days spent away from their families go on. In important ways, then, these holidays represent a reason for roving street vendors to go home to rest and to be with their children. Knowing that there is a fixed date on which they may be able to go home also helps them cope with the demands of the job while they are in Hanoi.

In addition to these holidays, the 1st and 15th days of every lunar month are important days on which acts of spiritual and ancestral worship are performed. They include the burning of incense and votive papers and the offering of ceremonial plates of fruit and other foodstuffs. For some roving street vendors, these days can represent a reason to go home if they are in Hanoi or to remain at home if they are not, but most of them see those two days of the month as an opportunity to make more money than usual and would prefer to be in Hanoi if at all possible. Some even switch from selling what they normally do to selling incense sticks and votive paper instead.

Ceremonial Rites of Passage

Weddings, funerals, and to a lesser extent the birth of a child are ceremonial rites of passage that also impose obligations of time and money on a roving street vendor. These obligations arise in two ways: when the street vendor must attend the ceremonies of others, and when she and her family organize ceremonies of their own. Weddings and funerals typically involve a ceremonial meal to which friends and family members are invited, and the cost to the family hosting one of these meals can often run into the tens of millions of dong. While it is the case, as discussed below, that a family hosting a meal will receive cash gifts from the people in attendance, these gifts are rarely

Loi returned from Hanoi 5 days before the death anniversary celebration for her husband to begin preparations...

Once she got home, she had to visit the home of each family she intended to invite to extend a formal invitation. Because her husband's relatives live far away, it was alright to use the telephone to invite them, but for people who live nearby, the telephone was out of the question. In all, 36 people (equivalent to 6 "tables") were invited. She also had to plan the meal, and for this she called on her sister to help because of her experience in this sort of thing. In the end, it turned out to be a very traditional ceremonial meal with an important exception. In addition to the customary plates of boiled chicken, pork intestines, fried beef, green vegetables, sticky rice, broth, fresh rice noodles, rice alcohol, and fresh beer, they decided to add three different dishes of dog meat. Loi explained that they made this break from tradition in order to please the guests.

On the day of the meal, Loi invited several people to come early to help with the cooking. For this particular meal, the men slaughtered the animals and chickens, and the women did all of the cooking. Once the food was prepared, a special plate with all of the dishes except the dog meat was placed on the family altar as an offering to her late husband. One "table" was served on each of the two beds located on either side of the house, one on the traditional wooden table in front of the family altar, and three were served on straw mats placed on the floor of the house. The meal began at 10am, and while it officially ended at noon, the last guests did not leave until well into the afternoon.

The total cost of the ceremony, including the cost of the meal she had to prepare the night before for five members of her husband's family who live far away and had to spend the night at her house, was VND2 million. When all of the envelopes were counted, Loi said that she received only VND1 million.

enough to cover the cost of the meal, and it is not at all unusual for the family to go into debt to pay for everything.

In addition to these financial costs, a street vendor hosting a ceremonial meal will usually have to come home several days early in order to prepare the meal and make other arrangements. She will often spend another day after the meal to clean up or just to rest. The opportunity cost, measured in terms of time lost by not working in Hanoi, can clearly be significant to a street vendor and her family.

The costs of attending wedding and funeral meals organized by others can also be significant. For ceremonies organized by friends and relatives, it is important that the street vendor's family be represented. In some cases, her husband can represent the family by himself, meaning that the street vendor may not have to return to her village if she is working in Hanoi. If the husband is in poor health or deceased, however, the street vendor will usually have no choice but to represent the family herself at the meal. Also, in the case of close friends and family relatives it is imperative that the street vendor attend the meal with her husband, even if it means returning on short notice from Hanoi. In some cases, she may also be expected to return home a day or two early to help out with the preparations. Once again, the opportunity cost of attending meals organized by others can weigh heavily on a street vendor and her family.

There are also direct financial costs of attending ceremonial meals organized by others. At wedding and funeral meals, each family that is represented is expected to give a cash gift commonly known as an "envelope".[28] There is usually no ceremonial meal for the birth of a child, but people are expected to give an envelope in this event as well. The amount of money given for each ceremony is determined according to village norms, and there is tremendous social pressure to adhere to these norms. It is extremely rare for a family, no matter what its financial status, to give less than the village norm, even if it means having to borrow the money. A family should also not give more than the village norm, as this would be viewed in an unfavorable light as showing off. Throughout much of rural society, just as families in dire economic straits are reluctant to make a public display of their own unfortunate circumstances, so too is the concept of modesty an important principle to which better-off families are expected to adhere.

While village norms vary, most street vendors report that the amount of the ordinary gift has gone up steadily over the past several years.[29] For many of them, the norm of VND10,000 in the late 1990s had become five times that much or more by a decade later.[30] For many street vendors, it would take about two days of working in Hanoi to make that sum. For ceremonies involving close family relatives, the amount that has to be given can be double the ordinary gift or even more. Since these latter ceremonies also require that a street vendor be present in her village, their cost is especially high. If she has to give a gift of VND100,000 and also be in her village for two or three days, the cost can easily approach the equivalent of a week's worth of work in Hanoi.

The number of weddings, funeral ceremonies, and births for which a street vendor must

In addition to time, Loi's ceremonial obligations also involve money...
Between our interviews with her in 2005 and 2006, Loi estimated that she had to spend approximately VND2.75 million on ceremonies. Wedding ceremonies were the most expensive and amounted to more than VND1,000,000. She gave VND300,000 for a nephew (the son of her brother) and VND100,000 for each of two other relatives. She attended a dozen other weddings for which she gave VND50,000 and three more which cost her VND30,000 each. She also spent VND300,000 on funeral ceremonies including VND100,000 for a cousin. She then spent VND50,000 for another funeral ceremony and VND30,000 each for five more people from her village who died. Death anniversary ceremonies, including transportation, cost her VND250,000, and these would have been more were it not for the fact that her step-mother did not organize a meal that year for the anniversary of the death of Loi's father. Loi also had to give several gifts amounting to VND100,000 to mothers of new-born infants.

Loi also expected that her ceremonial expenses would soon top VND3 million, since one of her brothers was building a new house and she planned on giving him between VND200,000 and VND300,000. Given that her daily profit from her street vending job was typically less than VND20,000 at the time, all of this meant that she needed to work more than 100 days in Hanoi just to pay for her ceremonial expenses.

give an envelope will vary from year to year, but the total amount of these expenses is almost always substantial. In villages where the norm was still in the VND25,000 to VND30,000 range, they rarely fell below VND200,000 per year and more often than not would fall somewhere in the range of VND300,000-500,000. In villages where the norm has already increased to VND50,000 per meal, the total amount that a family must give each year is clearly going to be higher.

In addition to all of these ceremonial rites of passage, a roving street vendor who happens to be in Hanoi must also return home to celebrate the death anniversaries of close family relatives. A death anniversary is one that all who were closely related to the deceased must attend, and there is no option for a street vendor to have her husband represent the family. These anniversaries include those of deceased members of her husband's family, and even when the husband himself is dead, a street vendor must continue to be present to celebrate the death anniversaries of his close relatives. Furthermore, she is expected to give a cash gift to the member of the family who organized the anniversary meal. This gift typically ranges from VND50,000 to VND100,000 for people who are not close family members of the deceased and to at least twice that for people who are. This, too, can sometimes represent as much as a week's worth of income for many street vendors.

The number of death anniversaries that a street vendor must celebrate will increase over time as she gets older and members her family and her husband's family pass away. As a result, the obligations of time and money that are associated with these ceremonies will

> **And finally...**
>
> In Loi's family, death anniversaries fall most heavily in the 4th, 5th, and 6th lunar months. The 9th day of the 4th month is the day of her husband's death. The 18th day of that month is the death anniversary of her father, and the 25th day is for the death of a cousin. Then, on the 10th day of the 5th lunar month she celebrates the anniversary of her father-in-law's death. That same month, she also celebrates the death anniversaries of her mother-in-law and an aunt. She has three more anniversary celebrations in the 6th lunar month: one for her mother, one for her husband's grandfather, and one for an infant child that she lost.

also increase over time. Furthermore, since there is no control over when these anniversaries take place, it is not unusual for a woman to have to return to her village several times each year in a relatively short time period. When this happens, the costs of time spent away from Hanoi as well as any cash obligations are felt even more acutely than they might otherwise be if they were spread out more evenly across the year.

The demands of time and money associated with weddings, births, funerals, and death anniversaries are also important in that they help shape and reinforce notions of mutual obligations and responsibilities among rural families. This is also true for a variety of other ceremonies that are held to mark important occasions in the life of a family, many of which will be discussed later on. In accepting a gift, a family implicitly assumes an obligation to reciprocate that gift at some time in the future. Alternatively, a family giving a gift may itself be reciprocating a gift that was received on a similar occasion sometime in the past.

As part of this system of reciprocal obligations, a family will typically keep track of which families it is in a "credit" position with and which families it is in a "debit" position with.

In Nga's village in Phu Tho province... whenever there is a ceremonial meal, everyone invited to that meal asks the others how much they are giving. This helps guarantee that everyone gives the same amount. Nga then explained that if she gives a gift of VND50,000 at the wedding ceremony of, say, her neighbor Mai, Mai would then have a gift obligation to Nga. If, by chance, Nga's mother-in-law were to get sick after that, Mai would be expected to give something, perhaps VND50,000 but maybe more or maybe less. This gift, however, would not reciprocate Nga's original gift to Mai but would instead confer upon Nga a new gift obligation to Mai. That way, when Nga's son gets married, Mai would still have an obligation to give Nga whatever amount people in the village decides is the appropriate amount. At this point, Nga would now have two gift obligations to Mai: one of whatever amount she received when her mother-in-law got sick and another for the gift she received for her son's wedding. In this way, she said, people go back and forth from "credit" to "debit" positions vis-à-vis one another.

In no way does this mean that a street vendor would be excused from attending a ceremony organized by a family with which she was already in a "credit" position, nor does it mean that she would refrain from accepting a gift from a family with which she was in a "debit" position. The social norms governing the exchange of these gifts would not allow it. Still, the very strong idea exists in the minds of virtually all of the women with whom we have spoken that they have certain obligations to people with whom they are in a "debit" position and that other people with whom they are in a "credit" position have certain obligations to them. For many, particularly those who find themselves in need, this means that a gift may sometimes be reciprocated outside of the normal ceremonial channels of giving and receiving. For a country like Vietnam, where there are few government safety nets provided to families like those of most migrant street vendors, this can be very important.

And when Thu's daughter got married in 2007...

Thu prepared a wedding meal of 60 tables for 360 people consisting of grilled pork, pigs feet, sauteed beef, chicken, sticky rice, a broth soup, and beer and alcohol. She said that after paying for this meal and for another meal of 20 tables the week before at which the future son-in-law visited the family to ask permission to marry her daughter, she had VND5 million more in expenses than what she received in cash gifts. Still, these gifts conferred a future obligation on her part to the people who attended the meals. Thu then said that until her daughter got married, she was able to remember her family's gift obligations but that she now kept a book that recorded each of the families from whom she had received a gift. She also mentioned another reason for starting the book: because she still has two unmarried children, it will help her come up with a guest list of people to invite when those two children get married. Coming up with that list of people with whom she has reciprocal gift obligations was difficult enough the first time, she said, and she does not want to have to do it again.

Education

Doi Moi and subsequent reforms have altered many rural family attitudes and practices, but perhaps none more significantly than attitudes about education. Even though virtually all street vendors born before *Doi Moi* came from families that were too poor to allow them to attend high school, they all want to see their children have at least the opportunity to continue their education through high school. Many of them say that if their children are able to finish high school and pass the university entrance exam, they will continue to do whatever they can to help them. This is not a trend that is isolated to street vendor families, and all the women say that in their villages, the majority of children now go on to attend high school. Part of the phenomenon is related to the increase in factory job opportunities that has come with the extraordinarily high growth rate of the Vietnamese economy over the past decade and because a great many factory jobs require a minimum of a high school diploma.[31] In an even more fundamental way, however, it is related to a change in the hopes and dreams that many roving street vendors have for their children. While very few of them see any possibility for themselves of escaping the lives they lead as farmers, almost all hope that their children will be able to do something else, and they see factory wage-labor employment as the best chance for their children.

The importance that is now attached to education is something that, just as it would have in the past had today's roving street vendors gone

> **Not many street vendors' children go on to university but...**
>
> Hao's 20 year-old daughter passed the entrance examination on her 2d try after Hao and her husband spent VND1 million on extra classes. Hao didn't want her to continue her studies, but her husband, who finished high school (Hao did not) encouraged her to go on. People in her village said that the family is already poor, so why would they let the daughter go off to university. Hao agreed with this view, even though she later said that she hoped the girl would finish. An additional worry was that if she did graduate, they would not have enough money to bribe the girl's way into a job. Her husband was fully behind the additional schooling, though: Hao explained that he's more "modern" than she is.

29

on to high school, has placed real hardships on rural families. Education expenses are typically cited as among the most important family expenses in the surveys we have done, and for many women, the principal reason that they started to work as roving street vendors was to be able to cover them. There are two types of expenses. The first are the official school fees which have to be paid in lump-sum payments every September at the start of the school year and usually again at the start of the second semester. The official fees include the national education fee that is determined by the state, but they also include fees that are determined by each commune to cover such budgetary expenses as classroom renovation, building supplies, and the like. They can, consequently, vary significantly by commune as well as by grade level, but they can easily reach the equivalent of more than an entire month's worth of street vending income for each child.

The second set of fees is unofficial and most notably includes fees that must be paid for supplemental courses. These are classes that are generally given by the teacher outside of regular school hours, and the teachers justify them by saying they will help children better learn the material they are supposed to learn in school. While some parents think these classes may be beneficial to their children, many view them as an act of extortion. Either way, because they feel that their children might receive a failing grade if they do not take these classes, most of the women say that they have no choice but to pay for them.[32] While the fact that the supplemental course fees are usually paid on a monthly basis may make them somewhat less onerous than if they were paid at the same time as the official fees, their impact on the family budget is rarely taken lightly.

Housing

Villages in and around the Red River Delta are characterized by a variety of architectural housing styles. There are still some thatch roof mud houses that remain, but most of them have been replaced by single story, peaked tile roof houses made of brick stucco walls that are known as "category IV" houses. A somewhat more recent design than the peaked roof house is also a single story house but one with a flat roof made of concrete. Even more recently, multi-story houses based on urban architectural designs have made their way into rural areas, and it is not at all uncommon for a village today to contain at least a few of these houses. The street vendors in this study are most likely to live in peaked-roof houses.

In traditional rural society, the house has long been viewed as the principal residential structure of the family, distinct from what are referred to as secondary structures. These structures are usually not attached to the house itself and include the kitchen, the toilet, storage sheds, and for some families, animal cages. With flat roof houses and even some of the newer houses, the distinction between principal and secondary structures has lost some of its importance since in many of these houses, the kitchen and even the toilet can be can be built inside or attached to the main part of house. In either case, the house, kitchen, toilet, and animal cages form part of the family compound, which is then surrounded by a fence or brick and concrete wall. The compound may also include any number of vegetable gardens, fruit trees, and perhaps even a fish pond, and because running water is virtually non-existent, it almost always includes a well.

The house itself has long been an important part of the cultural and economic space of the rural family. The inside of the house has a central room in which the family altar plays a prominent role. Here is where ceremonial offerings to the ancestors are made throughout the course of the year, and it is also where guests are received and special meals are served. On each side of the central room is a smaller room. These smaller rooms, which may or may not have inside walls separating them from the central room, are used as bedrooms, as places to store family tools and stocks of grain, and as places where income-earning activities may occur. The outside of the house is also an important economic space, for this is where families may plant fruit trees, grow vegetables and condiments for their own consumption, raise livestock and poultry, and in some cases dig fish ponds for raising fish.

Generally speaking, the houses in which most roving street vendors live are not large, and the living conditions for their families can often be quite crowded. This is particularly true for large families and for families that use a portion of the house for economic activities. In those cases where a street vendor is still living in the same house as her husband's parents, she and her family are usually relegated to one of the smaller rooms where they share the same bed and eat their own meals. The rest of the house is for her parents-in-law and any other sons or unmarried daughters living with them.

The Decision to Build a New House

Whether a street vendor lives in the same house as her in-laws depends on whether she and her husband have been granted the status of an independent household and on whether they are able to mobilize the resources to build a new house. Either way, it is generally expected that a young couple will eventually build a house of their own.[33]

The new house is often built on land that is part of the compound belonging to the husband's parents. This is because the residential area of most villages is surrounded by rice fields and secondary crop fields, as well as by rivers and dykes. With rural population growth, available residential living space in many villages has become limited, and the subdivision of family compound land has now become widespread.

The subdivision of the family compound has produced some important changes in the economic

> **After Thuy's husband finished his military service in 1987...**
> he came back to his village to join his wife. They and their two children, a daughter born in 1988 and a son born in 1990, continued to live in a small category IV house with his parents and one of his two brothers. Then, in 1997, Thuy and her husband were able to build a new three-room house with a concrete roof on a plot of land inside the family compound, land that had been used as a vegetable garden. The compound also had a fish pond, but this was filled in in 2004 so that the husband's other brother would be able to build a house to live in once he retired from the army. As a result, the compound now has three houses on it. Thuy says that each of them will eventually be walled in so that the three brothers and their families can live as three separate households, but this will not happen until her mother-in-law dies. As long as she is alive, the mother-in-law, whose husband is already dead and who now holds title to the land, will not hear any talk whatsoever of fragmenting the family compound into three smaller ones.

32

role that the compound now plays compared to what it played in the past. It is not uncommon for a family to have to clear some of the compound gardens in order to build a house, gardens which, as indicated earlier, are important in terms of helping a family meet some of its food needs. The loss of compound land for building purposes has at times also resulted in the loss of space for other activities, including animal and fish raising. However small all of this may seem, it has had the effect of further integrating many rural families into the market economy both in terms of meeting certain food needs and in terms of finding outside sources of income.

The pressure to build a new house does not come only from within the family itself. There is also a social pressure that results from the fact that the house, in addition to serving as a private space for the family, also serves as a public space through which a family is seen by the rest of village society. The economic reforms that transformed the rural family into the basic unit of agricultural production and that simultaneously imposed on each family the principal responsibility for its own economic well-being were, as noted previously, met with a tremendous amount of enthusiasm and support by the rural population. With this fundamental transformation of rural society, the house has increasingly become a window through which other people in the village are able to judge how well a family is doing. From our discussions over the years with roving street vendors, it is apparent that poverty, no matter what the causes, is

---

Ha got married at the age of 20 and moved to her husband's village where the two of them lived with the husband's parents...

They were eventually instructed to form an independent household, but they did this while continuing to live in the same house, a three-room tile roof house. They were given the smallest of the three rooms, which they now share with their two children. There is space enough only for one bed in the room. The house is old and in need of repair, but Ha has little hope of being able to make the needed repairs. Her husband is ill and cannot work, and the two of them are already heavily indebted. All of the money she makes as a street vendor is used to make interest payments on her existing debt and to meet the family's living expenses. Her one comfort, she said, is that there were still a number of families living in thatch roof houses.

---

something to which a certain amount of shame is attached. They say that they are not alone in thinking this way, and they go on to say that the house itself is looked at as perhaps the most apparent indication of a family's economic well-being. Many feel, for example, that families in their villages still living in thatch roof houses must really be very poor and in dire economic straits, for otherwise they would have surely found the means to build at least a tile roof house to live in. Those who say this also say that people living in these houses are undoubtedly aware of what others say about them. At the other extreme, they look at multi-story houses as a clear indication that a family has "succeeded" and is able to live a "comfortable life." What all of this means is that street vendors themselves feel a strong pressure to live in a house that gives the appearance of a family that, while perhaps not rich, is at least in line with village norms regarding living standards. This can include not living with the husband's parents for too long after being granted independent household status. It can also mean not living in a house that is too old or one that is in a state of disrepair.[34]

Constructing and Furnishing a House

For most street vendor families, the construction of a new house is the most important expense they are likely to incur. By the end of the 1990's, a new peaked-roof house typically cost around VND30 million. Over the course of the next decade, these costs increased dramatically,[35] and housing construction remains one of the principal reasons that a street vendor family goes into debt. However, it is rare for a family to build a new house without having spent many years saving money for it as well. The total amount saved can often be as much as half of the anticipated cost of building the house. For many families, these savings would not have been possible without the contribution from the income a street vendor earns in Hanoi.

Once a house is built, there is a steady stream of expenses that need to be made in order to furnish it. Most of these expenses are for basic necessities, but they are also important because the inside of the house as well as the outside serves as a "social window" on the family. The family altar consists of a wooden shelf attached to the rear wall of the central room of the house and a wooden chest of drawers placed below

34

it. Because of the religious importance that is attached to the altar and also because it occupies the central place inside the house and is seen by everyone who visits, the altar is usually the most ornate and expensive piece of furniture that a family owns. Families that can afford only a simple altar when they are young will often buy one with the idea of replacing it later with something much more elaborate.

Other household furnishings include at least one bed and a furniture set that usually consists of a low table, two chairs, and a straight-back bench on which people can either sit or lie. It is customary for parents to give their sons a new bed as a wedding present, so this generally does not have to be bought, but families with young children will often try to buy a second bed. The furniture set is placed in the central room in front of the altar. To save money, the furniture set can be made of plastic or metal, but because it is used to receive guests, fancier wooden furniture is preferred. Other high priority items include at least one lighting fixture in the central room, a portable electric fan, and large storage containers made of wood, metal, or plastic to store the family stocks of rice and secondary crops.

Once they meet these high priority needs, street vendors can focus their attention on a long list of other desired household purchases. These include a buffet to store dishes and teacups, and a dresser and/or an armoire in which to store clothing, a desk with a lamp for children to do their homework at, and a television. Along with a television comes the need for a DVD player and speakers in order to watch movies and sing karaoke. For many families, an electric rice cooker for the husband or children to use while the street vendor is in Hanoi has also become a high priority household item, but some families do not want to have to spend money on the rice cooker and then have to pay the electricity costs to use it. The same is true of a refrigerator: more and more street vendor families recognize the convenience of owning one, but many are not willing or able to incur the expense of buying and running it.

As a general rule, street vendors say that they do not go into debt in order to furnish their houses and prefer instead to use money from their current sources of family income. Of course, these needs must be weighed against other pressing needs of the family, including the need to pay off the debts they incur in order to build the house in the first place, so it typically takes a street vendor many years to furnish a house to her liking. Most of them believe that it would be impossible to even think about getting their houses the way they prefer without the money they make from their jobs in Hanoi.

The Effect on Others of Building a New House

A family's decision to build a new house can affect many people in a village. First, this is a time when the family building the house is certain to call in any loans it has made to other people in the village. Often, when a person needs to borrow money from someone in the village, the loan is made in the form of a gift obligation, somewhat analogous to the gift obligations that characterize much of the ceremonial gift giving practices. This will be discussed in more detail later on in the chapter,

---

When Loan got married in 1981...

she and her husband lived as part of his parents' household in Phu Tho province. When they were told to form an independent household six months later, they called upon family and friends to help them build a small house made of mud-brick walls and a thatch roof. They lived there until 2004 when they decided to build a new category IV type house with brick walls and a tile roof. At that time, Loan estimated that about half of the families had already built category IV houses, and half still lived in thatch roof houses. Still, she said that families like hers were feeling real social pressure to build a new house. She and her husband had saved 10 million of the estimated VND30 million cost of the new house, and construction began at the end of the year. They got another VND5 million from the sale of the piglets they had been raising. They planned to borrow an additional VND10 million from the bank with the remaining 5 million coming from brothers and sisters in the amount of VND100,000 each. The house took two months to build, but once it was done, they decided to tear down the old house and add a fourth room in its place. This added another VND20 million to the total cost of the house, and they paid for it in part by selling one of their two water buffalos, seven more pigs, and all of the family chickens. They intended to use this room as a storeroom until their older son gets married, at which point he will live there until he can build a house of his own. Then, when their younger son gets married, he will move into the extra room with his wife. Finally, it is expected that the oldest son will move back to live with Loan and her husband when they get old, and the younger son and his wife will move into the house of his older brother.

---

but what it essentially means is that the person lending the money does not want to be paid back until he or she needs it.[36] As a result, street vendors often find they are called upon to pay pack a portion of their outstanding debt on short notice, regardless of whether or not they are in a position to be able to do so. The construction of a new house by someone in the village is one of the reasons they can be asked to pay back a loan.

The family building a new house is also likely to call on other people in the village to lend it money to help cover its costs, either in the form of a "gift" or in the form of an outright loan. Most street vendors tell us that they are not really in a position lend out money for this or any other reason, and very often they do not. If the person asking for the money is a close family relative, however, it is much more difficult to refuse, even if it means that the street vendor and her husband have to go into debt themselves to help the relative.

Once a house is built, finally, it is the custom for the family to organize a housewarming ceremony to which relatives, friends, and neighbors are invited. Thus, even people who are not able or who are not called upon to lend money to help build the house do not always escape incurring some kind of expense in the form of a gift that has to be given at this ceremony.

Agricultural Production

For the overwhelming majority of rural farm families, the dissolution of the collective farming system was unquestionably the most significant aspect of the early *Doi Moi* period. What followed was a national program of land redistribution that allowed the family household to replace the village cooperative as the basic unit of agricultural production and distribution. This program began in 1988 with a provisional distribution of agricultural land (Resolution No.10 of the Vietnamese Communist Party) and culminated with the passage of the 1993 National Land Law. Under the terms of this law, families were granted land-use rights, which, for rice and other annual crop lands, were intended to last for 20 years. During this period, families were further granted the right to transfer their land-use rights through inheritance or through market transactions. Farmers were told that at the end of 20 years there would be another redistribution of agricultural land. This means that most roving street vendor families are still cultivating the same fields that were formally allocated to them in 1993. Most of them have not heard anything further about plans for the next land redistribution program, and there is no certainty in their minds about when or even if it will take place. If it does, almost all feel certain that, for demographic reasons discussed below, they will lose land compared to what they have now.[37]

Irrigated Rice Land Holdings and Yields

Generally speaking, street vendors say that the land redistribution program was accomplished fairly and equitably. The amount of land that an individual family received was based on family size, and in villages where differences in the quality or type of fields were significant, families were given proportionally equal amounts of each type of land.[38] Because of differences among communes in total land area and in population, the amount and type of land that each family member was allocated varied significantly from one commune to another. Among street vendors in this study, the amount of rice land allocated to each family member ranged from 0.5 to 2.0 *sao*, with the majority reporting that their families received between 1 and 1.5 *sao* per person.[39]

In the vast majority of cases, street vendors told us that children born after the 1993 Land Law did not receive an allocation of use rights to any land at all. The reason for this was that most communes allocated all of their irrigated

> **Hue's rice fields...**
> At the time of the last land distribution in 1991, Hue was already married. The distribution was determined on the basis of 1 *sao* of rice field land per person, but because she was born in a different village, she was only entitled to a plot of land in her native village and not in the village to which she moved after getting married. Still, she was able to swap her field with another woman from her husband's village who had subsequently moved to Hue's village after getting married. They received another *sao* of rice land after the birth of their daughter in 1994, but by the time that their son was born in 1997, the village had run out of land and was no longer allocating anything to families with new-born infants.

rice land at the time of the 1993 distribution, and there was simply no more land left. In some communes, officials did set aside some land to allocate to children born after 1993, but this was almost never enough land to last more than a year or two. As a result, there are many street vending families today whose per capita land holdings are less than what was allocated to them in 1993, and the number of families with less than 1 *sao* per person is now likely to be significant.[40] Equally important, it means that there many street vending families in which some or all children will not be entitled to any land when they get married, unless the next land redistribution actually takes place. Of course, if it does take place and is accomplished on the same principles of fairness and equity as the last one, virtually all families will end up with less land than they currently have. In the meantime, because the marriage age for rural women is now 18-20 years and for men a year or two older, young men and women who were born after the last land distribution and who have no land use rights of their own are already starting to get married.

All of these numbers confirm something that is widely acknowledged throughout the Red River Delta and surrounding provinces: rural families today simply do not have enough land to survive on rice production alone,[41] and for families that do not have some kind of supplemental income, the situation is only likely to get worse. Our own estimates, based on average rice yield and consumption figures provided to us by street vendors themselves, suggest that only those families with per capita land holdings of at least one *sao* are able to meet or exceed their own rice needs over the course of a year. Even those families that are able to produce a rice surplus, however, would not be able to use that surplus to meet all of their other food and non-food needs.

A further indication that families of roving street vendors may not produce enough rice is that the vast majority of them do not sell any of the rice that they do produce. In 2007, for example, only 28 percent of 203 street vendors surveyed said that they ever sold any of their rice crop. (Indeed, "never" is a word we frequently heard in our interviews when we asked a woman if her family ever sold any rice.) Even this number can be misleading because a family that does not grow enough to feed itself is often more likely to sell some rice than a family that

> **Hoa and her family have a total of 6 sao of agricultural land...**
>
> The land was distributed to the family in 1994 on the basis of 1.5 *sao* for her and her husband and 1 *sao* for each of her three children. This would normally be enough to feed her family for the entire year and to have enough left over to feed her animals, but because she needed money to meet her family's non-food needs, she often found that she had to sell some of her rice harvest. This, in turn, caused her to run out of rice during the 2nd and 3rd lunar months, right before the first harvest season. Now that her children are older and she can spend more time working in Hanoi, she no longer needs to sell as much rice and, consequently, no longer needs to buy any. She illustrated this by saying that three years ago she only had to buy rice in the 3rd lunar month and for the last two years hasn't had to buy any rice at all.

produces a rice surplus. Again using the data from 2007, 69 percent of families that do grow enough rice to feed themselves said that they do not sell any of that rice, but 21 percent of the families which do not grow enough rice said that they do sell rice. One reason for this is that rice-deficit families tend to be poorer than other families, so they frequently have to sell some rice to meet immediate cash needs, even if it means having to buy rice later at what is usually a higher price. In addition, many families, whether or not they grow enough rice, raise animals and need to use some of their rice to feed them. Finally, food security continues to be an important concern in rural society, and many of the street vendors who do grow enough food to feed both themselves and any animals they may be raising say that they would rather stock any rice surplus than sell it.[42]

Secondary Crops

Secondary crops also play an important role in village agriculture. The principal crops that roving street vendors say they cultivate are groundnuts, soybeans, maize, manioc, and sesame. Secondary crops are planted on non-irrigated fields and, in some cases, on irrigated rice fields after the second rice harvest in the fall. Non-irrigated fields are usually cultivated year-round, starting with a five-month planting at the start of the lunar year followed by two successive three-month plantings of various combinations of secondary crops.

While the vast majority of street vendor families cultivate secondary crops, the reasons why they do this vary. Generally speaking, these families can be sorted into four categories, each reflecting a different importance of secondary crop cultivation to a family's livelihood. The first category comprises families that grow secondary crops to provide feed for their animals. The principal crop grown for this purpose is maize, but manioc and other tuber crops can occasionally also be grown. Wherever possible, a family will grow maize on its own fields, but some families rent additional land for this purpose as well. The number of families also growing tuber crops is somewhat smaller, and we came across no families that rented any additional land in order to grow them. As a general rule, families that grow maize and tuber crops to feed their animals do not produce a surplus, so any revenue they receive from their cultivation comes from the subsequent sale of animals and not from the sale of these crops.

Another group of families plant secondary crops either for their own consumption or for small amounts of cash that can reach up to several hundred thousand VND. Frequently, these are families with small secondary crop field holdings of 1 *sao* or less per family, and they do not rent additional fields from their communes. Instead, they tend to rely on off-season cultivation of their irrigated rice fields plus whatever secondary crop field area they may have been allocated.

A third group of families lives in communes where, for reasons of terrain, there is limited or no irrigation. As a result, these families have at least some fields on which rice can only be grown during the rainy season, and they are forced to grow some other crop, usually groundnuts, during the first planting season of the year. Depending on the amount of land involved, the money earned can be significant, but it is usually not enough to offset the cost of rice that the family must buy because of the single rice-growing season. In that sense, these families are different from a fourth group of street vendor families that grow secondary crops primarily as cash crops from which they derive an important source of income.

The families in this fourth group are most likely to rent additional secondary crop fields. The profit from the sale of these crops usually falls somewhere in the neighborhood of VND1,000,000 per year. For most of them, this is a significant amount of money and an important reason why many women return home from Hanoi to plant and harvest secondary crops. At the same time, it is clearly not enough for any family to get by on and should be understood instead as only one of what are usually many sources of income on which migrant street vendor families depend for their survival.

The same rules that applied to the distribution of rice fields in Hue's village also applied to secondary crop fields...

but, because Hue had given her secondary crop field to her parents to cultivate, she and her husband only received the 1 *sao* of land to which he was entitled. Starting around 2000, however, she began renting 3 more *sao* of secondary crop fields from a nearby military camp. She grows groundnuts on these fields from the 1st through the 6th lunar months and follows this with successive 3-month plantings of sesame and then sweet potatoes. After paying VND200,000 per year to rent the fields, she is able to make a profit of VND1,000,000 from the sale of groundnuts and another VND300-400,000 from the sale of the other two crops.

Agricultural Calendar

The tasks that are required to grow both rice and secondary crops play a major role in how a street vendor allocates her time between Hanoi and her village. During the year, there are a number of peak labor demand periods that require a street vendor to spend a significant amount of time at home. The first of these is associated with the first-season planting of rice and secondary crops. Throughout the Red River Delta, this usually takes place during the first few weeks after the Tet holiday period.[43] Prior to transplanting, the rice fields have to be cleared and plowed, and seed beds have to be started. Any off-season secondary crops that were planted after the second season rice harvest in the fall also have to be harvested at this time of year. The fields on which these crops were grown then have to be plowed before they can be planted again, usually right after the rice has been transplanted.

Because Tet is a time when street vendors are home, it follows that this is one of the months in which street vendors spend the least amount of time working in Hanoi. However, the Tet period is when families are required to spend a significant amount of money on food, gifts, and clothing, so the first lunar month is also when many street vendor families encounter real hardships as the month progresses. Most street vendors, consequently, try to spend at least some time, often not more than a week, working in Hanoi. They let their husbands do much of the field preparation work and then come back home toward the end of the month to help with transplanting rice and planting the secondary crops they are growing.

The next peak agricultural demand period starts near the end of the 4th lunar month or the beginning of the 5th lunar month with the harvest of the first season crops. Almost immediately after the rice is harvested, the fields must be cleared and plowed again in preparation for the second season planting. At this time families also repair the small dirt walls built up around each field so that water stays in once the rice has been transplanted. Secondary crop fields also need to be harvested, plowed, and then planted again during this period.

Because the second season crops are planted immediately after the first season harvest, the labor demands during this period are greater than they are at any other time of year. It is not surprising then, that at this time of year street vendors tend to spend the most amount of time at home doing agricultural work. Depending on when the first season harvest begins, the work can often stretch out over a six-week period during the 5th and 6th lunar months, and during these two months more street vendors remain at home for the entire month than at any other time of year. However, most of them run into a similar kind of cash flow crisis that they run into during the planting period after Tet. Just as they do at Tet, many of them try to come to Hanoi at some point during this period in order to earn money. In 2006, for example, approximately one third of the street vendors we surveyed did not come to Hanoi at all during the 5th lunar month, but two thirds did. Of those who did come to Hanoi, there was a roughly even split between those who stayed for less than half of the month and those who stayed for more than half of the month. We found a similar pattern for the 6th lunar month, but slightly fewer women (25 percent) spent the entire month at home, and slightly more (56 percent) spent more than half the month working in Hanoi.

The last peak agricultural labor demand period begins with the second season's harvest near the start of the 9th lunar month. Because there are only two rice seasons in the northern part of the country, the fields do not have to be immediately plowed again and the labor demands are not as great as they are during the time between the first season harvest and the second season transplanting. Still, the rice has to be dried before storage, and the second season secondary crops need to be harvested, which can take two weeks or more. Families that grow off-season secondary crops must also plow their fields before planting them again, and street vendors from these families may spend a week or more at home doing this. Either way, fewer than 20 percent of the women interviewed in 2006 stayed home for the entire month in either of the 9th or 10th lunar months, and more than two-thirds of them spent more than half of the month working in Hanoi in each of those months.

Outside of these peak demand periods, the need for agricultural labor slackens considerably but by no means disappears. Throughout most of a growing season, particularly during the first growing season which takes place before the monsoons start, water has to be hand-pumped from the irrigation canals into the rice fields. This has to be done most frequently right after transplanting but usually takes place at least twice a week after that. Then, a few weeks before the harvest, water has to be pumped back out of the fields. Fertilizer has to be applied on at least three different occasions throughout the growing season, and pesticides have to be applied as they are needed. For some insects, this has to be done when the rice plants are pollinating, whereas for others it must be done between the time the rice kernels start to form and when the rice is harvested. Rodent damage is also a major problem, and it is not at all unusual for farmers to apply rat poison to their fields. At least once per season, usually a few weeks after transplanting, the rice fields also have to be weeded. Finally, even when work on the fields is not required, someone must visit them regularly to check on water levels and any sign of insect or rodent damage.

This must be done at least every four days, but many families visit their fields more frequently, sometimes every day. With the principal exception of pumping water, the same tasks that are performed on a family's rice fields must also be performed on the family's secondary crop fields, although not necessarily with the same frequency or doses.

Some street vendors rely on their husbands to perform most or all of these tasks, but most return home for at least a few days each month to help out. Our survey in 2006, for example, showed that 75 to 80 percent of street vendors spent at least one week at home during each of the months of slack agricultural labor demand. While there may be other reasons why they go home as well during these months, virtually all of them say that while they are at home they perform whatever agricultural work needs to be done.

Agricultural Expenses

There are a number of costs associated with agricultural production that have to be paid over the course of the two growing seasons. These include the costs of chemical fertilizer and insecticides as well as a number of government-imposed taxes and fees. For a limited but growing number of street vendor families who use hired agricultural labor to help them with their food production, the agricultural wage also needs to be included among the input costs these families incur.

The single greatest cost associated with agricultural production for most rural families today is the cost of fertilizer.[44] There has been a sharp increase in the price of fertilizer over the past several years, and many street vendors talk about the extra burden this has placed on their families. Since even a family with rice field holdings of 1 *sao* per person is not likely to sell much of their harvest, the cost of fertilizer has to be paid from some other source of family income. If the street vendor's family rice field holdings were 1 *sao* per person, and if she earned VND30,000 per day from her job in Hanoi, she would need to work from 15 to 30 days each season, or from one to two months per year, to pay the fertilizer costs for the family rice fields. If her rice field holdings were only 0.5 *sao* per person, the street vendor would have to work approximately 7-10 days each agricultural season to pay for fertilizer.

It is far more difficult to estimate the cost of insecticides because the types and amounts used vary significantly from year to year. Because of the urgency with which insecticides must be applied once insects start to appear, many street vendors tell us that their husbands have to borrow money to buy them and then wait for their wives to return from Hanoi before paying the money back.

In addition to the cost of chemical inputs, there are agricultural taxes and fees that farm families must pay at the end of each rice-growing season. Most of these charges are levied in terms of kilograms of paddy rice per *sao*, meaning that these costs vary from family to family and from region to region according to how much land has been allocated to a family. Some other taxes are paid on a per capita basis, and the amount that a family pays for these therefore depends more on family size than do the taxes determined on the basis of a family's land holdings. While not all of them are associated with a family's agricultural production per se, they are collected along with the agricultural taxes a family must pay, and it is difficult for most street vendors to separate them from their agricultural taxes.

The agricultural land use tax had been the most significant national tax imposed on farm families, but in 2003, in an effort to improve rural living standards, the government exempted most farmers (those with less than two hectares of cultivated land) from the tax until 2010.[45] Beginning in 2011, the land use tax does not apply to fields with at least one rice crop per year.[46] The residential land tax is determined on the basis of the number of square meters inside the family compound, and while it is not strictly speaking an agricultural tax, it is assessed in terms of kilograms of paddy rice and collected along with all of the other taxes and fees at harvest time.

The other taxes that a family must pay are local taxes. The most significant of these is an irrigation tax for each of the two rice-growing seasons. Most villages also have a field surveillance tax, and other local taxes may include a flood and storm prevention tax, various extension service taxes, a civil service tax, a contribution for national defense, a contribution for the families of war dead, local road construction fees, and health clinic fees. These taxes are also determined on the basis of a predetermined number of kilograms of paddy rice per *sao*.

Because there is so much variation in the amount of taxes a family pays, it is difficult to estimate what these might be for a typical street vendor family. Still, however large their taxes are, the income earned from working in Hanoi is what helps these families pay them. In this sense, taxes are one more reason why roving street vendors feel that they must go to Hanoi in order to maintain their rural identities.

Wage labor in agriculture is a fairly recent phenomenon in villages in and around the Red River Delta, and a growing number of street vendor families are now starting to rely on this type of practice. In 2007, for example, 17 percent of the women in our survey said that they use hired labor to help in their fields. For these families, the cost of hired labor must also be factored into their food production costs.[47]

One reason families hire agricultural labor is that they do not have a cow or water buffalo with which to plow their fields. These families often have no choice but to hire someone to plow their fields at the start of each growing season. Another reason why some families decide to hire agricultural labor is linked to the opportunity cost of time spent working on the family fields. For a roving street vendor's family, the opportunity cost here is the foregone income from her job in Hanoi. If the street vendor is in Hanoi and must return to her village to work on her fields, the cost also includes the cost of transportation to and from her village. Most street vendors are well aware of these costs, which is why an increasing number of them have begun to hire agricultural labor. The bulk of this hiring takes place at planting and harvest times. Finally, about half of the women who use hired agricultural labor decide to return home either to supervise the work or to help out themselves. Because the use of hired labor shortens the number of days required to perform each task, however, these women are able to go back to Hanoi sooner than they would otherwise.[48]

Animal Husbandry

Animal raising is another important agricultural activity in which roving street vendor families engage in order to generate revenue. Pigs are the most common animal raised, partly because they are kept in pens inside the family compound and do not require a lot of space. Of the 233 street vendors we interviewed in 2006, almost 60 percent said that their families raise pigs. Some families breed piglets, but most of them (77 percent) purchase young pigs to raise and then sell as meat pigs. They typically raise one or two pigs at a time, and while a few families are able to manage four sales per year, most of them are able to manage only two or three.

What is striking about pig raising is the number of roving street vendors who say that there is little or no profit to be made from this activity. In 2006, almost 30 percent of those families who did not raise pigs said that the principal reason for this was because there is no profit in it. In addition, almost 40 percent of the 128 families that did raise pigs reported that they made no profit.[49] If families do raise pigs, it is principally for two other reasons. First, pigs represent an important source of manure that most farm families combine with chemical fertilizers on their rice fields. The second and perhaps even more significant reason is that pig raising represents an important form of saving for many rural families. Each meat pig can typically generate a revenue of VND1,000,000 or more, an amount that all street vendors say they would be unable to save by putting aside a little money each week. Since many rural family expenses must be paid in relatively large lump-sum amounts, this kind of saving is an important part of their coping strategies.[50]

Livestock

Cattle raising is another important activity throughout the Red River Delta and surrounding provinces, but relatively few street vending families (only 7 percent in 2006) report that they raise cattle in order to earn extra income. Those who do usually raise one cow or bull per year, and the revenue they get can easily reach VND2,000,000 or more. They say that the profit on this is significantly higher than it is for pigs, primarily because the cost of feeding cows is far less.

Nonetheless, there are a number of reasons why most families do not raise livestock to sell. Many of them already own an animal that they keep in order to plow their fields, and they do not have the space inside the family compound to keep another. Raising cows also requires a significant amount of labor time since the animals can rarely be turned loose to graze. Many families cannot afford to spend the necessary time each day, and in the families who can, the children are usually called upon to perform this work. Finally, some women cite the significantly higher investment cost associated with the purchase of a young calf each year as well as the initial investment cost of building a pen in which to keep it as reasons why their families do not raise cattle as a way of earning extra income.

Poultry

A somewhat larger number of street vendor families raise poultry as a way of earning additional income: in 2006, just over 20 percent of families raised poultry, with most of them (almost 90 percent) raising chickens and the rest raising ducks.[51] Not included in these numbers are those families who raise poultry primarily for family consumption and not for profit. Even for these families, however, there is an advantage to keeping a few chickens or ducks that raising other animals or growing secondary crops do not have. This is that both live birds and eggs can

The avian flu epidemic that spread throughout Vietnam in 2004 also reached Hue's province of Phu Tho...

She said that the authorities ordered all poultry in a number of neighboring communes to be culled, but they did not order any cullings in her village even though many chickens in that village died. At the time, she had 5 grown chickens that survived, but all of the 400 chicks that she was raising died. She estimated her loss at VND1 million, half of which was money she invested in the chicks and half was profit that she would have made if she had been able to raise and sell the chicks. At this rate, once the flu epidemic was over and she was able to resume raising chickens, it would have taken her a full year simply to recover her investment cost of 2004 and another year after that before she could make any profit. Unfortunately, all of the chicks that she was raising in 2005 also died, this time from a disease that she says was unrelated to the avian flu virus.

be sold at just about any time of the year, thereby offering families the opportunity to generate small amounts of cash when needed.

However, poultry raising carries with it significant risks, and even before the first outbreak of avian flu in 2004, it was not uncommon for entire flocks to be wiped out by disease. Since 2004, virtually all of the women we have spoken with say that there has been at least one poultry culling either in or near their communes, and those women who lost their birds say that only people with much larger flocks than they are able to raise were entitled to any government compensation. While ongoing fears about avian flu have not convinced street vendor families to give up their practice of raising poultry, many of them have cut back on the numbers of birds that they keep while taking what they say is a "wait and see" attitude.

Whether performed as a source of income or as a source of saving, raising animals and poultry can be important to street vendor families. However, street vendors themselves are not the ones who will do most of the labor associated with this activity. If their families do have animals and poultry, it is because there is somebody else at home who can take care of them, at least during the times that the street vendors are in Hanoi working. The job of raising pigs is usually one that falls on the husband, while children are often the ones responsible for grazing cows and looking after the family poultry flock. For the street vendor herself, none of these activities constitute a convincing reason for her to remain in her village or for her to return from Hanoi on a regular basis and give up the income that she would make in Hanoi.

Debt

Debt plays an important role in the lives of many rural families, and the families of roving street vendors are no exception. It is one of the principal reasons that many of them begin migrating to Hanoi to work at this job, and it is an equally important reason why others continue to work at the job longer than they otherwise might. We have both anecdotal and empirical evidence to suggest that street vendors use the money that they borrow in constructive ways: to build houses, buy animals, cover emergencies, and invest in their own family enterprises.

There is, of course, another side to debt, which is the burden it can place on families hard-pressed to repay loans. While recognizing its value, in this chapter we want to focus on the pitfalls that debt can bring to rural families.

Incidence of Debt

Recent national surveys, the Vietnam Household Living Standards Survey (VHLSS) did not ask about overall indebtedness[52] but rather found that in 2002, 32 percent of "poor families" in the Red River Delta had borrowed money in the 12 month period prior to the survey[53] and that in 2004, 32 percent of all families had made debt payments in the previous twelve months.[54] In 2010, only 8.7 percent of rural Red River Delta respondents reported that they had either borrowed from or remained indebted to a preferential credit scheme.[55]

However, none of these figures is an accurate measure of the true extent of rural indebtedness. First, the number of families officially classified as "poor" within any given village is only a small fraction of the total number of families in that village, and it should not construed that only families officially designated as "poor" find themselves having to go into debt.

Second, as we discuss in more detail below, families who borrow money in any given year typically take more than one year to pay the money back, even if, as in the case of bank loans with relatively short terms, they are forced to roll over their debt through borrowing from family relatives and other private individuals. We have found in our own work that unless it is specifically asked about, much of the borrowing from relatives is not thought of as debt per se and tends to go unreported. Finally, not having made a payment in the prior 12 months does *not* necessarily mean that the household has no debt, something that will also be discussed in more detail later on. All of this suggests, then, that at any given time, the percentage of all rural families having borrowed money that year is likely to be well above the figures contained in the VHLSS reports, and the total number of families having outstanding debt from prior years is likely to be even higher.

Our own observations suggest that this is certainly the case with roving street vendor families. Over the years, we have found that on the order of 70-80 percent of these families have either recently been in debt, were in debt at the time of the survey, or had been planning to go into debt sometime in the near future. In 2007, for example, 68 percent of the more than 200 women with whom we conducted street surveys reported that their families were in debt at the time of the interview. When we add families that were not in debt at the time of the survey but who had been in debt at some point during the previous 12-month period, the number increases to 81 percent.

In 2003, Hoi was a 45 year old widow who had an outstanding debt of VND10 million... that she owed to relatives and other people in her village. She incurred this debt as a result of three things that happened in 2002. First, her son had a bicycle accident. Second, the village raised the level of the road in front of her house, and she had to raise the floor of the house in order to prevent flooding. Finally, she needed money to rebuild her pig pens.

This was the first time she had incurred such large debt, and she came up with a plan that she hoped would enable her to pay it off. She calculated how much land she would need to grow enough white rice for her family, and then she borrowed some additional land that she intended to use to grow sticky rice. Her plan was to sell the sticky rice that she grew on the land that was not necessary for her family's needs and use the proceeds to pay off her debt. Even though the people she had borrowed from told her that she could wait until the price of sticky rice went up, she planned to sell the entire harvest immediately so that she would not take advantage of her lenders.

Reasons for Going Into Debt

The main reasons for going into debt are for housing construction, child rearing and general living expenses, investment in animals, major medical expenses, and, as will be discussed in more detail later on in the chapter, debt rollover. Of these, the most commonly cited reason is housing construction. In 2006, for example, we found that more than twice as many street vendor families borrowed money to build or renovate a house than for any other reason. Animal raising is actively promoted by the government as a key component of its overall poverty reduction strategy, and loans for this purpose are widely available. While we have found that far more families say they want to borrow money in order to raise animals than actually invest in this activity once they get the money, it should not be surprising that loans actually used for this purpose are also important. In 2006, a total of 23 percent of indebted families had borrowed money to invest in either pigs or some other form of animal raising.

Many street vendor families also find that they have to go into debt after the birth of a child. This is usually because they are poor and because they cannot rely on money a woman might otherwise make as a migrant street vendor to cover the cost of child rearing and other living expenses. Education fees, some of which fall due in lump-sum amounts at different times of the year, are another reason some street vendor families have to borrow money. Minor medical expenses are usually treated as out-of-pocket expenses or are covered by short-term loans that are paid back as soon as possible. Medical expenses that require long-term borrowing usually involve hospital care for a family member or long-term medical care for that person at home. Some of these are related to old age and involve a street vendor's own parents or her parents-in-law, but medical emergencies can happen to any family at any time. Debts of this kind are often the most crippling for a family.

In addition to the many reasons for going into debt described above, the vast majority of street vendor families are also forced to borrow small amounts of money that they pay back in a relatively short period of time. In 2006, for example, more than 75 percent of the 227 women said that either they or their husbands incur short-term debts of this sort. Most of the time (76 percent) the amounts that they borrow are VND50,000 or less, and they usually borrow from the same one or two people each time. The most common reason for this kind of borrowing is to buy food and meet other daily living expenses. Minor medical expenses, supplemental course instruction fees, and ceremonial gift obligations are the other principal reasons for short-term family debt. Often, the husband has to borrow the money while his wife is working in Hanoi, and she pays it back when she returns. Many women say that this kind of borrowing is a fact of village life for them, and while the amounts are small, a debt of VND50,000 can nonetheless represent more than a day's income from her street vending job.

Loi says that she and her husband struggled with debt almost from the day they got married in 1976...

Before she became a street vendor in 1996, her husband migrated to do a number of different jobs that included working in a brick factory worker, working' as a carrier in the Dong Xuan market in Hanoi, and after that burned down in 1994, selling laundry detergent from a bicycle out near the Perfume Pagoda in what was then Ha Tay Province. During that time, Loi stayed home to look after their two children, but her husband was able to bring home very little money from any of these jobs and their debt kept mounting. When they finally made the decision that Loi would start coming to Hanoi to work, the debts that she could remember amounted to VND10 million, most of which was used to buy a plot of land and to build a thatch roof house when they first got married and a tile roof category IV house many years later. This amount did not include an additional VND5.6 million that they borrowed that same year to lend to Loi's brother so that he could invest in a brick factory in Hung Yen, money that he was unable to pay off after a seasonal flood turned all of his unbaked bricks to mud.

Over the next eight years, the couple was able to reduce their outstanding debt to around VND2 million, largely the result of Loi's working in Hanoi, but then, in the 7th lunar month of 2004, her husband became ill and she had to spend almost all of her time at home to take care of him. His health took a serious turn for the worse in the 11th month of that year, and after several stays in different hospitals in Hanoi, he died five months later. To cover the cost of his medical treatment and the subsequent cost of his funeral ceremonies, Loi had to borrow more than VND18 million, meaning that her total outstanding debt stood at more than VND20 million.

Loi was determined to pay all of these debts off before she would allow herself to think about giving up her job as a street vendor, a job she said that there was nothing to like about. She was also determined not to incur any further debt, but this did not happen. She continued to find other reasons for which she needed to borrow money, most notably for housing renovations intended to make it more comfortable for her husband's relatives who live far away and have to spend the night at Loi's house each year for his death anniversary celebration. She also needed to borrow money in 2009 to take care of her mother-in-law for three months while she was ill and to pay for her funeral expenses after she died. Still, with some help from her son who had gotten a job as a factory driver in Hanoi, Loi had managed to pay off much of her outstanding debt and said that as long as her health held out, she hoped to be able to pay it all off in just a few more years. Unfortunately, her back gave out on her at the end of 2009, and at the age of 56 Loi had to give up her job as a street vendor and return home to her village.

Sources of Lending

Rural families borrow from a number of official and unofficial sources. Unofficial or informal sources include family relatives, close friends, neighbors, professional moneylenders, and other village acquaintances. Official sources include banks and other government and non-government institutions. Loans made by these institutions are usually associated with poverty reduction and micro-credit lending programs.

In 2001, Nga's son was hit by a car while attending a local festival in Phu Tho province with his grandmother...

He was rushed more than 100km to the German Friendship Hospital in Hanoi where he had most of his foot amputated. The hospital costs alone amounted to VND14 million, and the family also had to pay for their son's medication and meals as well as for their own transportation, meal, and lodging expenses during the two months that he was hospitalized. To pay for all of this, Nga sold all of the jewelry she had received as a wedding present and then borrowed VND10 million from relatives at no interest. They also were given VND4 million in cash and VND3 million in foodstuffs from the driver of the car.

Several months after the accident, Nga's family received an official classification as a "poor family" and was able to borrow an additional VND10 million from the government's Poverty Eradication Program. Her husband had to sign a letter stating that he would use the money to invest in livestock, but knowing that their son would now be unable to work as a farmer, they used the money instead to buy a milling machine for him to make money with when he gets old enough to use it..

Nga also became a basket lady after her son's accident. She decided to come to Hanoi to work instead of working as a carrier at a nearby brick factory or in the port, mostly because she was afraid she would spend her earnings every day and would be unable to put anything aside if she stayed at home. By working in Hanoi, she only spends money on food and lodging for herself and is able to bring home relatively large amounts of money all at once. Most of this is used to help pay off the family debt.

As for the milling machine, one of only two in the village, Nga helps her husband out with it when she is at home. Unfortunately, when she first started using it, she got her hand caught in the flywheel belt and had to have part of her index finger amputated. It cost her VND1 million, and she now jokingly refers to it as her million dong finger.

The Bank for Social Policies and the Bank for Agricultural and Rural Development are the principal institutions through which most lending programs are administered,[56] but some individual communes also administer their own lending programs. For example, we found one commune in Hung Yen province in which the local Women's Union lends up to VND1 million each year to a woman who is determined to be in dire need.[57]

Official loans have relatively short fixed terms. Depending on the lending program, these can be as long as five years, but terms of only one year are most common, at least among street vendor families. The principal is usually paid at the end of the term, but interest, with rates ranging from 0.5 percent to 1.5 percent per month, is paid either monthly or quarterly. Land use certificates, commonly referred to as family "red books" are required as collateral for these loans.[58]

Although the terms of official loans tend to be short, many women say that they are able to roll over these loans when they come due. They do this in either of two ways. One way is to borrow money from friends and relatives and use this money to pay off the loan at the end of its term. Once the bank loan is paid off, they can then apply for a new bank loan and use this money to pay off the friends and relatives. A much more common practice, at least for the roving street vendors we have spoken with, is to roll over official debt with unofficial debt. When a bank loan comes due, they ask someone else, often a sibling or relative, to apply for a new bank loan. They then borrow that money from the sibling and use it to pay off their own bank loan. This effectively involves transferring the legal responsibility for the original bank loan to another family member, but the important thing for the women who do this is that the immediate pressure on them to pay back the loan is significantly eased. In many cases, they even lose track of when, how, or even if the person who allowed them to roll over their original loan was able to pay off the bank when his or her own loan came due. All they know is that they will have to pay that person back at some point in the future.

Women often say they can get around another problem with official bank loans, which is that because most of these loans are associated with a specific program, many of the reasons why they need these loans are not valid reasons. However, they typically claim in the application that they will use the money for its intended purpose. This is especially the case with micro-credit loans for animal raising, which, as indicated above, are readily available throughout the region. In these instances, many women declare that they want to borrow the money to invest in animal raising, but they fully intend to use the money for housing construction, emergency medical expenses, or some other purpose. They say that the commune officials are usually aware of this, and in some cases the officials even tell the street vendor or her husband what to put down on the loan application form. Part of the reason they may turn a blind eye is that the family land use certificate is required as collateral, but some women also feel that the officials are aware of and often sympathetic to the plight that has driven them to request the loan.

While there is no question that official lending sources are important both to rural families in general and to street vendor families in particular, our own data suggest that at least for street vendor families, unofficial sources of lending are even more important. This is illustrated in Table 2.1, which shows the incidence and type of debt held at any time during the 12-month period in 2006-7 prior to the time the survey was administered. The numbers reflect the 81 percent incidence of debt mentioned earlier.

The first thing that is important to note in Table 2.1 is that more than half of all families surveyed had borrowed money from both official and unofficial sources, clearly an indication of the importance of both types of lending sources. Among the remaining families that had incurred debt, however, borrowing from unofficial sources was more common: three times as many families borrowed only from unofficial sources as families who borrowed only from official sources. Looked at somewhat differently, just over 73 percent of all families borrowed from unofficial sources, while the number of families that borrowed from official sources stood at just under 59 percent. As further indication of the relative importance of unofficial lending sources, slightly less than 70 percent of street vendors said that given a choice, they would prefer to borrow from unofficial sources.

Table 2.1: Incidence and Type of Debt: 2007

	Street Vendor Families	Percent
No Debt	39	19.2
Borrowed Only From Official Sources	15	7.4
Borrowed Only From Unofficial Sources	45	22.2
Borrowed From Official and Unofficial Sources	104	51.2
Total	203	100

Borrowing from relatives is the most common type of unofficial debt, but street vendor families also depend extensively on non-family members when they need money. This can be seen in Table 2.2 which shows the incidence and type of unofficial debt for street vendor families for the same 12-month period in 2006-07. Only slightly more than one-quarter of these families did not owe at least some money to unofficial sources during this time period. Of the remaining families, very few (just under 5 percent) had not borrowed at all from family members. The rest of them (67.5 percent) owed money to relatives, but more than half of these families also owed money to other individuals who included friends, neighbors, professional moneylenders, and other village acquaintances.

Table 2.2: Borrowing From Unofficial Sources: 2006-07

	Street Vendor Families	Percent
No Unofficial Debt	56	27.6
Borrowed Only From Relatives	64	31.5
Borrowed Only From non-Relatives	10	4.9
Borrowed From Relatives & non-Relatives	73	36.0
Total	203	100

Although relatives may on rare occasions charge interest on the money they lend, it is far more common that they charge no interest. There is also no fixed term to these loans, and street vendors either pay them back as they are able or when they are asked to. We can discern no general pattern concerning interest on borrowing from friends, neighbors, and other village acquaintances, but when interest is charged, it is usually set at the prevailing bank rate. Professional moneylenders, on the other hand, typically charge rates that are much higher.[59] Friends, neighbors, and other village acquaintances will sometimes ask that the loans be paid back by a specified date, but they usually allow these loans to remain outstanding for several years or more. Professional moneylenders are also less likely to attach a fixed term to the loans they make as long as the interest payments are made on time.

The fact that most unofficial debt does not have a specified date when the money must be repaid means that the period of indebtedness associated with these types of loans tends to be significantly longer than with official loans. For the majority of families, this is one of the perceived advantages of borrowing from unofficial sources, regardless of whether or not interest is charged.

The absence of any fixed term to lending from relatives and other individuals, however, can also be a disadvantage. This is because many people who lend money do so as a form of saving, and even though they may not charge interest on the money they lend, they only want the loan to be repaid when they need the money themselves. It often happens, consequently, that a family that is in a position to pay back the money it owes will be told by the people who lent it to them that they do not need it. For many families, any money not accepted for debt repayment will be spent on other pressing family needs, so street vendors say that they often do not have the money to pay back a loan when it is finally called in. This causes them to roll over many of their loans, usually from other unofficial sources and to remain in debt longer than they otherwise might.

This particular form of borrowing resembles the system of reciprocal gift obligations that characterizes many of the ceremonial expenses for a family. It is most common for money that is borrowed to build a house, but it can be associated with borrowing for medical emergencies and other reasons as well. The way it usually works is that the person lending the money will tell the person who needs to borrow it that money is a "gift" rather than an outright loan. Of course, the person who accepts the "gift" understands that he or she will have to reciprocate at some point in the future when the original lender announces a need for the money. As previously discussed, not knowing when a loan will have to be repaid

In Hue's village in Phu Tho…

when a family is in need of a large sum of money, not only can that family ask that gift obligations owed to it be paid back, it can also decide to announce a general call for new gifts. These gifts can be given either in cash or in kind, but gifts in kind, as for example chickens, are usually given by people who do not have a lot of cash on hand. These gifts are usually sold by the family calling for the gifts, but the obligations created by accepting this kind of gift are reciprocated at some later date by an identical gift in kind.

The terms of reciprocity for cash gifts are somewhat more complicated. Here, a person making the cash gift must, at the time the gift is given, specify a non-cash good in which the gift is to be denominated. For example, if a person gives a cash gift of VND5 million, this person may specify that it is to be denominated in bags of cement. When the gift is reciprocated at some later date, the family that had received the original VND5 million gift must calculate how much the corresponding amount of cement would now be worth, thereby determining how much money must be given in order to repay the gift.

Hue recognizes the importance of this system to the way of life in her village, but unfortunately, she says that there are some people who try to manipulate this system for their own gain by taking advantage of such things as seasonal price fluctuations. When she and her husband built their new kitchen, for example, they received gifts that ranged in value from 50kg of rice (VND250,000) to a maximum of 2 tons of cement (VND1,500,000). These included twelve gift obligations that were owed to her and four new gifts, but they also turned down more than one new gift because they didn't trust the motivations of the people who offered them.

is a drawback to this type of borrowing that is widely recognized by street vendors, but many of them say that it is minor compared to borrowing from a bank. They say that while it is often easier to borrow large amounts of money from banks, the fixed and relatively short terms of these loans make it difficult for them to pay back all of the money at once. If they borrow from informal sources, they can borrow the same total amount by taking out smaller loans from many different lenders. This way, the odds of everyone calling in their loans at once are extremely small.

However, not all unofficial lenders engage in the practice of only wanting to be paid back when they need the money, and those who do not offer another advantage to migrant street vendors. Vendors say that banks have fixed payment dates on which principal and/or interest must be paid, and they do not accept payments except on these dates. Therefore, there is an advantage to borrowing from unofficial lenders whom they can pay as soon as they return from Hanoi with the money they make from street vending. If the timing of fixed payments is such that the vendor has the money to pay but the payment is not due, there are often too many other family needs to allow vendors to put the money aside. As a result, they may not have the money on the day that the bank requires it.

The Burden of Debt
The burden of debt on many families is related to the reasons that they go into debt in the first place. Debt can be both planned and unplanned, but even in the case of planned borrowing, most of the money that is borrowed is not used for investment purposes that could generate future income and help a family repay the debt. In 2006, for example, fewer than 30 percent of families in debt had used at least some of the money they borrowed for what could even remotely be considered investment purposes, and much of what could be called investment involved a significant risk of not making much profit.[60] This is not a critique of the borrowing patterns of street vendor families. There is nothing wrong, for example, with a family wanting to build a new house to improve its living conditions, nor is there anything inherently wrong with a woman who borrows money to help raise her children because she is poor and

Ha's first child, a daughter, was born in 1992, several months premature and weighed only 1.4kg...

The daughter had to be hospitalized immediately after she was born and continued to have health problems throughout her early childhood. As a result, Ha and her husband went into debt early on in their marriage. Her husband got a job as a motorcycle taxi driver in Hanoi while Ha stayed at home to take care of her daughter and a second child, a son, who was born in 1997. The husband was unable to make much money at this job, so in 2000, once her son was 3 years old, Ha started coming to Hanoi as well. Until then, the family had been unable to pay off any of the VND6 million that they had borrowed to pay for the daughter's medical expenses.

Then, in 2003, her husband fell ill, and after being brought home in the middle of the night in severe pain, was brought back to Hanoi the next day to see a doctor in Bach Mai Hospital where he was diagnosed with kidney stones. After three months of recovery at home during which he was unable to pass the stones, Ha took him to the German Friendship Hospital in Hanoi for surgery. His recovery from the surgery was difficult, and a set of X-rays two months later revealed that not all of the stones had been removed. His condition remains weak, and he is no longer able to work in Hanoi and can only perform limited agricultural chores at home.

As a result, Ha's job as a street vendor is the only source of income for the family, and she must balance her time carefully between time spent working in Hanoi and time spent back in her village where she is the principal farmer as well as the caretaker for her husband. At the same time, she has been unable to use any of the money she makes as a street vendor to pay off her family debt, which, after her husband's illness, had grown to VND13.5 million. While she has been able to roll over most of this debt into loans without any fixed term, it is hard to see how she will ever be able to escape this crippling burden of debt. By 2005, missed interest payments had caused her debt to rise to VND15 million. That year, she would have had to spend half of the money she earned in Hanoi simply to pay the interest on her outstanding debt, but this would have left her little income to meet her other family living expenses. The fact that by the end of that same year she had been unable to make enough money to buy fertilizer for her rice fields and had also been unable to pay for her children's supplemental school fees was a good indication of this.

they are too young for her to leave home to work. Instead, the borrowing patterns highlight the need for additional family income, some of which could be used to pay back the loans. Migrant street vendors try to meet this need with their jobs in Hanoi.

For many families, the burden of debt is also due in part to the unplanned nature of the debts that they incur as a result of medical emergencies. For street vendors, these expenses can easily lead to debts of from VND5 to 20 million, and they can also be associated with a sharp drop in family income if it means that either the street vendor or her husband cannot work for a significant period of time. Even for families that are relatively well off, sudden debts of this magnitude can be crippling, and a recurrent theme in virtually all of our interviews was concern about what these debts could do or what they have already done to a family.[61]

The burden of debt is further compounded by extremely high interest rates. Even for families officially classified as poor, the lowest interest rate available is six percent per year. Bank loans for families not classified as poor are very often set at 1.5 percent per month. Because the majority of street vendor families are not officially classified as poor, they typically must pay interest of up to 18 percent per year on loans from official sources. Not surprisingly, this turns out to be impossible for many families. Depending on the amount of the loan, some families manage to make their monthly interest payments but are unable to put money aside to pay back any principal. Others find that they are unable to make all of their monthly interest payments, much less pay back any principal. The first group of families winds up staying in debt for years, while the second group winds up falling further into debt each year.

Finally, another reason that makes it difficult for families to get out of debt is that many loans, including most bank loans, are not amortized. Instead, a loan is typically paid back in one lump sum either at the end of its term in the case of a bank loan or when the person is asked to pay it back in the case of many other loans. In the meantime, when interest is charged, people make only the interest payments. For families that are already having difficulty making their interest payments, paying off the entire principal at once becomes virtually impossible.

The most common response to these problems is for families to roll over their debt when it becomes due.[62] While debt rollover allows them to remain in debt for what often amount to long periods of time, it is not seen as a permanent solution to their problems. Most of the families included in our study were able to make at least occasional payments of principal and/or interest on their outstanding debts. Furthermore, virtually everyone we spoke with who was in debt talked about the intense personal and social pressures that they felt to somehow pay off their debts. Even those street vendors who had gone several years or more without making any payments of either interest or principal and who had no idea how or when they might get out of debt were unwilling to admit that they might never be able to do so.

Family Living Expenses

Daily living expenses, unlike the some other expenses we have already discussed, require a steady stream of income, and most street vendors, particularly those whose husbands work only in agriculture, say that they try to meet these expenses with the money that they make in Hanoi. Each time they go to Hanoi, they have a good idea of how long they will be there, and before they go, they try to leave at least enough money to cover the anticipated living expenses. If, as often happens, they cannot leave enough to last the family during their absence, they may send money back from Hanoi with bus drivers, motorcycle taxi drivers, or other people from their villages who happen to be returning home.

Family meals are the principal daily living expense. The two most important, and hence expensive meals of the day are lunch and dinner. Breakfast usually consists of either stir-fried rice, if there is any left over from the previous night's dinner, or a bowl of rice noodles. Lunch and dinner typically consist of three basic dishes that make up a traditional Vietnamese meal: rice, a "salty protein" dish of meat, fish, eggs, or tofu, and a leafy green vegetable broth. Except for important ceremonial meals, families almost never eat beef or chicken, and pork is the most common meat they eat. This is because pork is much cheaper than either beef or chicken, and even families that raise their own chickens generally prefer to sell them rather than eat them themselves. Even so, very few street vendor families are able to afford to eat pork every day, and even on those days when they do, they tend to buy the cheapest cuts. Otherwise, they try to eat a serving of dried or fresh fish, eggs or tofu. Most or all of these foods also have to be bought. They also have to buy a number of staples, the most important of which are MSG, fish sauce, soy sauce, salt, sugar, and other spices. Because of the flavor and the cost, many families prefer to cook with lard rather than cooking oil, so they buy a kilogram or so of pork fat at a time, which they then render and use over a period of up to two weeks.

In 2007, almost all of the women included in our study reported that they were spending between VND10,000 and VND20,000 per day on these village living expenses. These figures do not include the value of the rice that families produce and consume, nor do they include any spending on rice that some of them must make at different times of the year when their own stocks run out. Nonetheless, the figures do suggest that the basic diet of street vendor families is not extravagant. As stated above, most families do not eat meat every day, and the meat that they do buy usually has a lot of fat on it. In fact, many families may eat meat only once or twice week. Poorer families may only eat pork once or twice a month, usually on ceremonial occasions such as the 1st and the 15th days when a meal should be prepared and offered to the family ancestors. Otherwise, they often go without the salty protein dish entirely and eat a mostly vegetarian diet consisting of rice and a leafy green broth.

A way of putting these expenses into perspective is to look at them in relation to what a street vendor makes from her job in Hanoi. It is common among street vendor families that her job in Hanoi is the only source of family income that comes close to providing a regular flow of income. Now consider the hypothetical example of a roving street vendor who in 2007 made an average profit of VND30,000 per day and whose family living expenses at home that year were VND20,000 per day. It might appear that this family could have used the VND10,000 that would remain, but that is not likely the case. If that street vendor were working an average of 20 days per month in Hanoi, her profit for the month would have been VND600,000. This averages out to an income of VND20,000 per day, meaning that she would have had no money at all left over from her job in Hanoi to pay for her family's other expenses, including those for ceremonies, fertilizers and insecticides, education fees, and any outstanding debt. Her family's options, then, would be to try to meet these other expenses from money her husband makes, to increase the amount of time she spends working in Hanoi, to go into debt, or to reduce her family's village living expenses. In all likelihood, it would be some combination of these.

Of course, for a woman with an average profit of more than VND30,000 per day, the burden of meeting her family's daily village living expenses would be smaller. For example, a woman making a profit of VND50,000 per day and working 20 days per month in Hanoi would have an average daily income of VND33,000. This would leave her VND13,000 per day or about VND400,000 per month to pay her other expenses. Looked at in this way, it is easy to understand why even many street vendors who make a much higher profit than others say that they too have difficulty in making ends meet. At the same time, the majority of street vendors were making a daily profit of VND30,000 or less in 2007, and for these women, the fact that they migrate to Hanoi in order to make money does not, in and of itself, suggest that their families are able to lead very comfortable lifestyles back at home.

Conclusion

Virtually all street vendor families undertake a wide variety of agricultural activities. Most, however, do not have sufficient land to survive on food production alone, nor are they able to sufficiently diversify their agricultural activities–into significant increases in animal husbandry, for example–to eliminate the need for non-farm income.

While migration can be one solution to the problem of rural families needing more income, village life also imposes a variety of burdens and constraints on the ability of street vendors to earn income in Hanoi. Vendors are pulled back to their villages for important ceremonial obligations during the year, for agricultural tasks that need to be performed, and to simply be with their families and to rest. This results in a form of circular migration in which street vendors must balance the sometimes conflicting needs to be at home in their villages and to be in Hanoi making money.

One of the reasons that street vendors do this job and not others is that they lack sufficient education and training for other jobs. For many of them, continuing in school was a luxury that their families could not afford, and others dropped out in order to help out around the farm. With a median educational attainment of having completed secondary (middle) school, street vendors are handicapped in their ability to participate in the modernizing sectors of Vietnam's economy.

In their villages, there is pressure on street vendors not to shame their families by violating cultural and behavioral norms as well as pressure on them to conform to village consumption norms so as not to give the appearance of being poor. These norms impose significant financial costs that range from the cash gifts given at ceremonial meals to the need to have a good house. The gifts given on ceremonial occasions are part of a complex system of reciprocal gift obligations in which it would be unthinkable not to participate, while the renovation of an existing house or the construction of a new one is likely to be the most significant expense they incur over the course of their lifetimes. We do not suggest that in the absence of this pressure to avoid appearing poor, street vendors would choose to live in poverty, but the need and the desire for a better life is, along with their many other financial obligations, one of the main reasons they need to work in Hanoi.

Finally, the most important trap into which street vendor and other rural families fall is debt. In the country as a whole and for street vendors, too, formal lending sources have become more important in recent years, but we find that street vendors also use informal sources to an important degree. Through this combination of formal and informal borrowing, we are able to understand how those families who do not have enough money to get out of debt are able to get by for what are often long periods of time. Now we turn to the street vendor family decisions to migrate and the importance of the income they earn in Hanoi.

CHAPTER 3

THE DECISION TO MIGRATE

Although circular migration is, for the most part, a relatively new phenomenon that began during the *Doi Moi* period, the patterns of this form of migration, as we showed in the previous chapter, are now characterized by a set of rules that have become rooted in village custom and tradition. These rules affect the balance that a woman strikes between her job as a roving street vendor and the more traditional role of a woman as a child bearer and care provider for her children. While these rules may vary widely among villages and regions, they strongly influence how a woman thinks about herself in these multiple roles and how she is viewed by the rest of the village as she performs them. The same rules that help shape women's roles as both migrants and mothers also shape the patterns of family migration between a street vendor and her husband. In some cases, the patterns of family migration involve husbands who also migrate in order to find work. In the remaining cases, the husbands remain at home and work only in agriculture or at non-agricultural jobs in or near their villages.

In this chapter, we look first at our empirical data to show how important the incomes that street vendors earn in Hanoi are. The economic theories of internal migration that we cover in the appendix to this book home in on the need for and the expectation of earning higher income in a city, which is the reason that we begin with that issue*. Then we examine how families reach the decision for a woman to migrate to Hanoi to work as a roving street vendor in light of the other roles that she is expected to play at home. Part of that issue is a discussion of why she decides to come to Hanoi to work instead of doing something else nearer to home. We also look at the different patterns of family migration involving a street vendor and her husband and at how the family deals with the issue of child care in each of these patterns. Because husbands do not migrate in the vast majority of street vendor families, we also look at the reasons why the street vendor and not her husband is the one to migrate. Finally, we take a close look at the divisions of family responsibilities that arise both when a woman is working in Hanoi and on those occasions when she returns home.

The Importance of Income Earned in Hanoi

Inadequate income is the underlying reason why virtually all roving street vendors decided to migrate to Hanoi to work. Many of their families are already in debt by the time they start going to Hanoi, while others find that they simply cannot meet their village living expenses without at least one source of non-agricultural income. We showed in the previous chapter that, in addition to daily living expenses, there is a steady stream of other expenses that must be met at different times of the year, many of which must be paid in relatively large lump-sum amounts. We also showed that the family land holdings, including the holdings of families which are able to produce a rice surplus and the holdings of families which grow secondary crops, are insufficient to allow them to meet these expenses from food production alone. While animal raising is another agricultural activity that is important to many families, most of them say that this activity alone is not enough for them to meet all of their cash needs.

In this section, we summarize some of our previous work that showed in more detail the importance of informal sector income to the families of roving street vendors.[63] To do this, we use our survey results from

---

* Readers who are interested in learning more about the literature on migration should read the appendix to the book. In it, we briefly look first at some of what has been written from a theoretical perspective about migration. We also discuss in more detail much of the empirical literature about temporary migration in Vietnam. Doing this allows us to place our findings in the context of other work.

2000 and 2003 in the context of national data for Vietnam. We conducted our first systematic study of street vendor incomes in 2000 as part of a survey that included 168 circular migrants. In 2003, we conducted a similar survey that included 179 circular migrants. In each of those surveys, we asked about the money a woman made over the course of the previous year. The survey conducted in 2000, consequently, obtained income data from 1999, and the survey in 2003 asked about income earned in 2002. The results from those surveys are included in Table 3.1.

On working in Hanoi...

"Hanoi is a very lively city," Dung, a 43 year old street vendor from Bac Giang province, told us, "but I only come here so that I can earn enough money to survive. I don't pay attention to what goes on here…to whether people are rich or poor. None of that interests me. All I care about is earning enough money to get by and support my children. Otherwise, we would all rather be back in our native villages. Life is much better back home."

"My husband is ill and has to stay at home to look after the children and our pigs and chickens," said Lan, another street vendor from Hung Yen province. "Of course I would prefer to be at home so that my family could all be together and I could take care of my children. But life at home is hard, and I have to come. Otherwise, nothing compares to being at home"

"Just a few more years," Lan's husband tells her, "until the children are grown up. Then you can stay at home with me. It won't matter if we are poor."

Table 3.1: Street Vendor Take-home Income

Year	Number of Days Worked	Take-home Income per Work Day	Annual Take-home Income	Annualized Daily Take-home Income
1999	191	VND10,500 ($0.75)	VND2,005,500 ($143)	VND5500 ($0.39)
2002	216	VND14,500 ($0.95)	VND3,132,000 ($205)	VND8500 ($0.56)

Exchange rates: 1999 $1=VND14,000; 2002 $1=VND15,300[www.Vietcombank.com]
(Numbers have been rounded to nearest VND 500)

As illustrated in Table 3.1, we estimate that the annual income for a street vendor in 1999 was VND2,005,500 ($143 at the prevailing exchange rate). This figure is based on a median income per day worked of VND10,500 and an average number of days worked of 191. Because the women included in this study spend part of their time in Hanoi and part of their time in their villages, we also calculate a street vendor's annualized daily income, which shows how much of her income is available to a street vendor and her family on a daily basis throughout the entire year. We arrive at this figure by dividing the annual income by 365. In 1999, the annualized daily income was VND5500, or slightly more than half of what a street vendor was able to make on the days that she spent working in Hanoi.[64]

Table 3.1 also shows a significant increase in street vendor incomes between 1999 and 2002. Part of this increase was due to an increase in the number of days spent working in Hanoi to 216 (an increase of 13 percent), and the rest was the result of a 38 percent increase in the income per work day to VND14,500. The annualized daily income increased by 55 percent to VND8,500. While still quite low, all of the income figures for 2002 had risen much faster than the rate of inflation, which means that the real income that street vendor families were able to make was significantly higher in 2002 than in 1999.

One way to illustrate the importance of the incomes shown in Table 3.1 is to look at how these incomes could affect poverty among rural families. In the 1990s, Vietnam had two definitions of poverty: food poverty, based on the income necessary to consume a daily requirement of 2,100 Kcal per person, and basic needs poverty, which adds to the food poverty

> **Hoi became a basket lady in 1983 and says she still remembers the exact date...**
>
> She had gotten married at the end of 1982 and continued to work in the local embroidery cooperative until it dissolved a few months later. Shortly after that, on the first day of the 6th lunar month, her mother-in-law instructed her and her husband to begin their own household and to begin preparing their own meals. The young couple did not have enough food, and they were hungry all of the time. Finally, on the 24th day of that month she decided to go to Hanoi to begin selling fruit.

threshold the cost of other non-food necessities. We consider two hypothetical examples, one for 1998 and the other for 2002. A family of four living at the food poverty level of consumption in 1998 would have had, with the addition of the income earned by the average street vendor, an increase in consumption of 39 percent. This increase would have raised the family from the food poverty level to the basic needs poverty level. Similarly for 2002, adding the average street vendor's income to a family of four living at the food poverty level would permit an increase in consumption of 58 percent, raising that family 14 percent above the basic needs poverty level.[65]

These examples illustrate how the money earned from a street vending job could contribute to moving a rural family out of poverty or to keeping it out of extreme poverty. The fact that 18.3 percent of the rural population in 1998 lived at or below the food poverty line and 44.9 percent of the rural population lived at or below the basic needs poverty line only serves to underscore the importance of this point.[66]

Another way of looking at the importance of a street vendor's income during this period is to look at it in terms of the distribution of income or consumption for the entire population. Again, we consider two hypothetical cases. First, we assume a rural family of four in which the woman does not have an outside source of income. Then we look at what would happen to this family in terms of the distribution of income (2002) and consumption (1998) if we were to add the money that she could expect to make if she were to work as a roving street vendor. In the second case, we assume a rural family of four in which the woman already migrates to Hanoi to work as a roving street vendor. We then consider what would happen to that family if for any reason she were forced to give up her job. In each case, we use the average annual income that a street vendor made first in 1999 and then in 2002. Furthermore, in order to examine what would happen to a family's standard of living if it were to gain or lose this income, we assume that it is living at the mean level of income for each quintile of the population.[67] Given these assumptions, Table 3.2 measures the change in a family's standard of living in terms of how it would move across consumption quintiles in 1998 and income quintiles in 2002.

It also shows the percentage change that the addition or loss of a street vendor's income represents from the mean of each quintile of the distribution of income for each year.

Table 3.2: Living Standard Changes for a Rural Family of Four

	National Distribution of Consumption/Income*				
	poorest quintile	second quintile	third quintile	fourth quintile	richest quintile
1999					
addition of street vendor income	+1 quintile	+1 quintile	+1 quintile	+1 quintile	~
loss of street vendor income	~	-1 quintile	-1 quintile	no change	no change
change (+/-) from quintile mean	42%	27%	21%	15%	7%
2002					
addition of street vendor income	+1 quintile	+1 quintile	+1 quintile	no change	~
loss of street vendor income	~	-1 quintile	-1 quintile	no change	no change
change (+/-) from quintile mean	54%	33%	24%	17%	8%

*1999 refers to national distribution of consumption; 2002 refers to national distribution of income.

This table shows that in 1999, except for families already in the richest quintile of the population, the addition of a street vendor's income would have moved most families into the next-highest quintile. In 2002, adding street vendor income would move most families in the lower three quintiles up into the next quintile. Table 3.2 also shows that standard of living gains would have been highest in families in the two poorest quintiles. In 1999, a family living at the mean expenditure level of the poorest quintile would already have been living below the food poverty threshold. A woman's decision to start working in Hanoi as a roving street vendor would have increased that family's level of expenditure by 42 percent and moved it into the second quintile, just eight percent below the expenditure mean of that quintile. If the family had been living at the mean expenditure level of the second poorest quintile, it would have moved into the middle quintile with a 27 percent increase in its per capita level of expenditure. In 1999, gains for families in other quintiles, while somewhat less, would still have been significant: families living at the third and fourth quintile means would have jumped up one quintile with per capita expenditure increases of 21 percent and 15 percent, respectively.

In 2002, a family of four living at the mean level of per capita income in the poorest quintile would have experienced an increase in income equal to 54 percent. This would have moved it to only six percent below the mean of the second quintile. Similarly, a family at the mean of the second poorest quintile would have seen a 33 percent increase in per capita income, moving it to four percent below the mean of the third quintile. The income gains for families living at the means of each of the other quintiles would have been 24 percent, 17 percent, and eight percent, respectively.

In Table 3.2 we also see that the loss of a street vendor's income would move most families in the second and third quintiles down one quintile in both 1999 and 2002.[68] Looking first at 1999, the magnitude of the decrease in a family's standard of living would be such that the average family in the poorest quintile would

Ways that basket lady income helps...
Hue and her husband have no outstanding cash debts, and the only current debts were ceremonial or gift obligations to other people in the village. When they built a new, three-room house in 2000, they used money that they had saved from selling animals and money that her husband made from his job as a mason, but they also had to borrow money. After Hue started working in Hanoi, they were able to pay off the amount that they had borrowed.

Also, before becoming a basket lady, Hue often had to borrow small amounts of money, and she would pay off these debts with money from selling their animals. Since she became a basket lady, Hue does not need to borrow money like this anymore, unless her children get sick and she needs to buy medicine for them. She says that since becoming a basket lady, most of her money has been used to pay off her debts. Once these are paid off, she wants to build a new pen to raise pigs in, but she also thinks that she will soon be in a position to be able to start saving money for her children.

living would be such that the average family in the poorest quintile would fall 45 percent below the food poverty threshold and 61 percent below the basic needs threshold. Families that began at the mean of the second quintile would find themselves in the poorest quintile, only five percent above the food poverty line but 25 percent below the basic needs poverty level. Even a family that began at the mean of the third quintile would, after experiencing a loss of a street vendor's income, fall into the second quintile and find itself only 4.5 percent above the basic needs poverty threshold.

In 2002, a street vendor family living at the mean income level of the poorest quintile would have had an income about eight percent above the food poverty line. However, if it lost its street vendor income, that family's income would have fallen to about one-half of the food poverty level. The family that began at the mean of the second quintile would end up in the poorest quintile after the loss of income; it would remain 18 percent above the food poverty line, but it would be 15 percent below the basic needs poverty level. A family that began at the mean of the middle quintile would fall into the second quintile but remain above both poverty lines.

The conclusions reached from the above examples assume that street vendor families either did or would make the estimated annual incomes shown in Table 3.1. Actual incomes either above or below these amounts would have an obvious impact on how much a family's standard of living might change, as would family sizes different from the hypothetical family of four used here.

> Thanh and her husband lost their agricultural land to an industrial park that was built in their commune...
> She got a job as a street vendor, and he found work as a local construction worker. While working at this job, her husband fell and broke his neck. He spent three months in the hospital and another three months at home before he died. Now, Thanh returns home every night to be with her three children, the oldest of whom was about to start high school while the youngest was about to enter 1st grade. She went heavily into debt when her husband went into the hospital, but the only money she makes is from her job as a basket lady and virtually all of this is needed to support her children. "It's hard" she said, "but I'm doing the best that I can."

up the job of selling foodstuffs on the streets of Hanoi would have a significant impact in both absolute and relative terms on that family's standard of living for all but the richest families. Similarly, if a street vendor were forced to give up her job, the loss of income from that job, particularly for families in the lower half of the distribution of income, could be devastating.

From our subsequent surveys, we know that daily incomes for street vendors have continued to rise: in 2006, typical daily income was VND20,000, while in 2008 it was VND25,000, and most recently, in 2010, it was just under VND35,000. Thus, from 1999, typical daily income more than tripled (from VND10,500 to VND34,900), while the price level slightly more than doubled during the same period.[69] Clearly, roving street vendors have benefitted from a rise in their real income, adding additional support to the claims about the importance of this type of income in aiding poverty reduction.[70]

Why Not Work at a Job Closer to Home?

When answering the question of why street vendors decide to migrate to Hanoi to work instead of working at jobs closer to home, most of them say that there are no other jobs in or near their villages and that they have no choice but to migrate. Many of them do not live close to any of the industrial zones that are being created by provincial and district authorities (only 14 percent of the women surveyed in 2007 lived in communes where any factories had been built in the previous ten years), and even if they did, they do not have the education or skills typically needed for these jobs. They also tend to come from villages in which there are few, if any, other job opportunities for women. In 2003, for example, more than 80 percent of the street vendors who worked as circular migrants said that they had never even looked for a job in or near their village, and 60 percent of those who had not said that there simply were no jobs outside of agriculture to look for.

Where local job opportunities for women do exist, street vendors typically say that these jobs are either too hard for them to do or that they do not pay enough for them to get by. Traditional brick factories, for example, have been widespread throughout the region, and many women did indeed work in them, primarily as carriers responsible for bringing uncooked bricks into the kilns for baking and then carrying the bricks out of the kilns once they have finished firing.[71] The way women were paid for this job made it difficult for them to take a rest if they were tired from carrying the heavy weights that are required of them. Brick carriers were employed by the factory owner as a team, and the team was paid not by the hour or by the day but by the total number of bricks carried into and out of the kiln for each firing. If a woman was unable to keep up with the pace of the team and needed to rest, other members of the team would do more work for the same amount of

---

Thu has two daughters, both of whom were able to find factory jobs...

The oldest daughter, Huong, worked as a seamstress in a garment factory in Hung Yen, but she was fired after only seven months when an internal audit revealed that she had not even completed 9th grade. At the time she was fired, she was still an apprentice and was paid only VND200,000 per month plus food and lodging. Eventually, however, she would have made around VND1 million per month, so she asked her family to try to buy a diploma for her from the school back in her village. The school refused, so Huong came to Hanoi to work with her mother as a basket lady.

Thu's younger daughter, Van, tried her hand at three factory jobs before she, too, decided to become a basket lady. Her first job was in a sock factory right on the outskirts of Hanoi where she was paid by the piece. She quit after only 12 days, in part because she was forced to work an extra shift from 6pm to midnight every other day. She said that the factory was too noisy and that she had started getting severe headaches. Van and a friend then went to Hai Phong where they got a job in a burlap bag factory, but she only lasted two weeks at this job because she could not learn how to make the bags. Finally, she found a job in a sweater factory on the outskirts of Hanoi. This time, she was fired because she was too short to use the loom properly and made too many mistakes.

Van, Huong, and Thu now all live together in a mezzanine built into the ground floor room of a house near the Long Bien market. They pool their money and keep it locked up in a small box. They know this is risky, but don't want to carry that much money with them when they are out on the streets. They also cannot leave the money with the landlady because she is dead, and they do not trust the landlord because of his gambling habits.

---

money. Women we have spoken with say that by working in Hanoi as roving street vendors they do not have to carry as much weight, and because they are self-employed, if they need to rest they do not wind up hurting anyone else.

Perhaps the other most common type of local job opportunity for women is to sell goods in rural markets, and many street vendors have in fact worked at this job during times when they have been unable to migrate to Hanoi. Very few of them, however, can rely solely on their own agricultural output for the goods that they sell, and they must buy from wholesale merchants instead. They usually sell these goods from bicycles or from fixed places in the local market. Either way, they say, the volume of sales and the markup that they are able to get are low, and the money they can make is nowhere near what they can make by migrating to Hanoi.

Once the decision to migrate to Hanoi is made, it is almost always with the intent of becoming a roving street vendor. An important reason for this is that most of the women are already married when they decide to go to Hanoi, and there are very few jobs that married women can work at and still return home on a regular basis. Many of the jobs in Hanoi's informal sector that are performed by women, such as sellers in shops and market stalls, restaurant workers, domestic servants, or karaoke bar singers, masseuses, and other types of sex workers are all jobs that require long-term, if not permanent migration to the city. They tend, consequently, to be performed either by single women or by women who marry but whose husbands and children live with them in Hanoi. The job of a roving street vending job is different and therefore attractive to many married women who need to migrate but who also want to maintain their rural family identities.

The decision to become a roving street vendor is influenced by the village norms and social networks that are an important part of rural life. The norms governing domestic migration in many if not most villages throughout the region are such that a woman would rarely be permitted to leave her village to go to Hanoi alone, nor would she be permitted to go there without knowing in advance where she was going to stay and what she was going to do. Instead, if she does go to Hanoi, she is expected to go as a member of a group of other women from her village who are already working there. The members of the group will then teach her the job of selling in Hanoi, arrange for her to live with them in their boarding house, and generally look after her while she is in the city.

Also at play here is the idea, very important in village culture in and around the Red River Delta, that people tend to follow the example of others in their village. Thus, it is rare today to find just one group of women from a village or commune migrating to Hanoi without finding several other groups of women in that village or commune migrating there to do the same thing.

> **Hue decided to start coming to Hanoi in 2002 after talking with her husband's sister...**
> Her sister-in-law was the first woman in her village to migrate to Hanoi and work as a basket lady. When she told Hue that she was able to make VND600,000 in 20 days, Hue compared this to what her husband was able to make as a mason, and she decided to become a basket lady. Her sister-in-law brought her to Hanoi and taught her the job.
>
> Since that time, 18 more women, all relatives or people from the same village, have joined Hue's group. They stay in the same house when they are in Hanoi, and while they sell separately, they usually leave the house together in the morning to go to the market and then fix a time and place to meet before returning at the end of the day.

Of course, a woman's decision to migrate to Hanoi depends on more than the fact that her family may be poor and that there may be no jobs in or near the village for her to do. It is influenced in important ways by her reproductive roles within the household as both a wife and mother as well as by the various gender roles that are attributed to men in different villages throughout the region. It further depends on the availability of job opportunities for her husband, either in or near their village or in farther away places that might require that he too migrate.

Why is it the Woman and not Her Husband Who Migrates?

There are a number of reasons that street vendors give to explain why they and not their husbands are the ones to migrate. Many of these reasons vary by village and by region, but others do not and appear instead to be rooted in more widely held beliefs and practices that cut across regions. In addition, within any one family, there are usually several reasons behind the decision that the wife be the one to migrate, and it is often difficult and not terribly useful to try to identify a single most important reason for this decision. We can say, however, that the need for income alone cannot explain the gendered nature of migration within the families of most roving street vendors. Once the decision for a woman to migrate is made, it typically means that her husband will remain at home and not migrate himself. Among those street vendors interviewed in 2006 and 2008, for example, only 15 percent (62 out of 410) had husbands who also migrated.[72]

Custom and tradition appear to play an important role in shaping this decision. Many women say, for reasons they cannot fully explain, that in their villages men simply do not migrate and that women instead are the ones who are expected to migrate if their families need extra income. More often than not, they see this part of a set of village norms whereby men tend to do what other men in the village do while women do what other women do. The very nature of these norms, consequently, tends to reinforce over time patterns of family migration in which husbands stay at home while their wives go to Hanoi to work. A number of women have told us that even if they wanted to stop working in Hanoi, their husbands would be reluctant or even unwilling to migrate on their own instead.

Another reason for the wife and not her husband to migrate is that in many villages, women say that more local job opportunities exist for men than for women. This is particularly important for street vendor families that depend upon two outside sources of income. In these cases, women often feel they have no choice but to migrate, whereas their husbands do have a choice. While some of their husbands decide to migrate anyway, most do not. Among the women interviewed in 2006 and 2008, 15 percent had husbands who also migrated, but 20 percent worked at jobs that allowed them to return home at the end of the day. The jobs that non-migrant husbands typically do are within easy walking or bicycling distances from their homes. They include work as brick cutters in nearby brick factories, as carriers unloading sand, cement, fertilizers, and other goods that are transported by boat to the many river ports throughout the Red River Delta, and as construction workers, usually as bricklayers and masons' assistants. By working at jobs in or near their villages, they are often able to return home at lunchtime where they can keep an eye on the children. Furthermore, because many of these jobs tend to shut down for several weeks during planting and harvest seasons and because there are usually many other opportunities to stop work as needed, the men who perform them can continue their jobs as farmers as well.

In addition, there is the perceived advantage on the part of many women of being able to make money every day as a street vendor, while many migrant jobs at which men work pay only at the end of the job. Some of these jobs, particularly those involving construction work, can last for several months, and families often need to depend on a more frequent source of outside income in order to meet their cash needs. Also, if a construction worker needs to return home before the end of a job for a family emergency, he usually only receives enough money to cover his transportation expenses. Street vendors, on the other hand, have far more flexibility. They make a cash income every day, and they can work or not without having to ask anyone else for permission.

As we noted in Chapter 2, their children's education is very important in street vendor families, and this importance also shows up in the patterns of child rearing within street vendor families. The ability to go on to high school is not simply a matter of being able to pay the supplemental fees each year so that a child can move on to the next grade. There are exams at the end of each year, and there is also the high school entrance exam that is given at the end of 9th grade, which not everybody passes. Parents understandably feel that children who do not do consistently well in school each year are less likely to do well on the entrance exam. Because of this, street vendors say that they take studying and doing homework far more seriously for their children than they ever took it for themselves. It is not surprising to hear them speak of the need to impose strict discipline on their children to make sure that they do their homework. It is also not surprising, given the culture of gender in rural society, to hear them say that their husbands are far better than they are at imposing discipline on their children.

This does not mean that the widely held view of the father figure as disciplinarian is the only or even the principal reason why the husband stays home to look after the children while his wife migrates to Hanoi to work as a roving street vendor. In most cases, it is not. This reason, however, has to be understood in light of the fact that the overwhelming majority of basket ladies say that, given a choice, it would be better for the mother to be at home to take care of her children than for the father. This is not to say that some women do not actually believe that their husbands are better at disciplining their children. It does suggest, however, that for many women, the notion that their husbands are better at disciplining their children is something that is used more to justify why the women migrate than it is to actually explain why that decision was made. In Chapter 4, we show that there is very little about the job that they like, and many of them try to find some comfort in this particular notion of why they must do it.

Similarly, in 2006, many women told us that their husbands stayed home because they were better at farm work. While this may be true in individual cases, it probably also reflects a particular understanding of "appropriate" gender roles, or it may also be an after-the-fact rationalization for her migration instead of his.

Another widely held and important idea that is used to explain why men remain at home is the belief that women can make and/or save more money than they can. Sometimes, this is because men are paid less money per day than women can make by working as street vendors, and in other cases it is because the jobs performed by men are more irregular in terms of the number of days worked. In the vast majority of cases, however, it is because street vendors say that if men were to migrate, they would spend a lot of their money on themselves for things like cigarettes, alcohol, gambling, and, while they are usually unwilling to speak of their own husbands in this way, other women. Women, they say, care more about their children and about seeing to their family needs than men do and for this reason are much better about saving money than their husbands.[73] Our own data suggest not only that street vendors do save most of what they earn when they are in Hanoi but that what little they spend on themselves while they are there does not afford them a very comfortable lifestyle at all. We discuss this in some detail in the next chapter.

Being away from their homes and family for what can often amount to weeks at a time imposes a heavy burden on roving street vendors. In our interviews with them, they often talk about how much they miss their children when they

> **When Thuy started working in Hanoi...**
> Before 2003, Thuy would come to Hanoi each month anywhere from two weeks to a month at a time. She missed her two children terribly, and often when she finished work early would want to go home to be with them and take care of them. But there were no buses at the time that went anywhere near her village, and she could not. Then, in 2003, the other women in her group found that the police crackdown against street vendors leading up to the SEA Games was just too much for them, and they gave up the job and returned to their village permanently. For Thuy, the idea of spending her nights in Hanoi alone, away from her family and in a house with other women who were total strangers, got to be too much for her as well, but she could not afford to give up her job. Instead, she decided to commute to Hanoi on a daily basis using an old motorcycle her husband had recently bought. At first, she had no idea how to even start the motorcycle, much less make it run, and she was terrified once she got it on the road. It only got worse for her once she got to the Long Bien market in Hanoi and then had to carry the weight of all of the fruit she bought each day on the back of her bike through all of the city traffic. After a while, however, she got used to driving it, and she says she is much happier being able to spend time each day with her children and (now) her grandchildren.

are in Hanoi. It is also not unusual for them to cry when they talk about this, both out on the street when they are surveyed and inside during in-depth interviews. When we asked in 2006 whether it would be better for the children if the street vendor or her husband were the one to stay home and take care of the children, 85 percent of the respondents said that they should be the one to stay home. If they do feel the need to migrate to Hanoi in order to work, it seems clear that they would rather be at home with their families.[74]

Migration and Child Bearing

A woman's decision to migrate to Hanoi to work as a roving street vendor is constrained by her reproductive role within the family as child bearer. Given this role, we discern three distinct patterns of migration with respect to when a woman decides to become a roving street vendor. The first is that she begins to migrate before she starts having children. The second is that she begins to migrate while she is still having children, meaning that she starts to migrate sometime after the birth of her first child but before the birth of her youngest child. The third pattern is that she waits until after she has finished having children before she begins to migrate.

The majority of street vendors who work as circular migrants fall into the third category and do not begin to migrate until they have finished having children. There is some indication, however, that this practice may be changing and that more women are now be starting to migrate sooner. This can be seen in Table 3.3, which includes data from 586 roving street vendors interviewed between 2000 and 2003 and data from 573 street vendors interviewed in 2006, 2008, 2009, and 2012. This table shows a drop in the overall percentage of women who begin to migrate sometime after they start having children and a sharp increase in the percentage of women who begin to migrate before they start having children. Women who wait until after their youngest child is born dropped from 62.2 percent in the period 2000-03 to 51.5 percent in 2006-2012. The percentage of women who started to migrate while still having children also fell in 2006-12, decreasing from 18.4 percent to 17.3 percent. For the same time period, the percentage of women who said they started to migrate before having any children at all increased from 19.4 percent to 31.2 percent.

While most women still wait until after they give birth to at least one of their children, the numbers contained in Table 3.3 do suggest that the need for an outside source of income is even greater now for rural farm families than in the past. From the data collected in 2006 and 2008, we also found that women who were already working in Hanoi when they became pregnant continued working, on average, well into their fourth month. Only 16 percent stopped working right away, and 23 percent continued working into their last month of pregnancy.[75]

Table 3.3: When Street Vendors Begin to Migrate

Year	Before First Child Was Born	While Still Having Children	After Youngest Child Was Born
2000-03	19.4%	18.4%	62.2%
2006-12	31.2%	17.3%	51.5%

There is no single pattern for when women either begin or resume working in Hanoi after giving birth to a child. For women who wait until after their youngest child is born before they decide to migrate, the median age of that child when they do start going to Hanoi is three years.[76] At this point, the child is old enough to be sent to nursery school, a practice that is not uncommon among street vendor families. Women who wait longer than this before deciding to migrate often wait until the youngest child is old enough to attend elementary school. More than two-thirds of street vendors who had not previously worked in Hanoi had started doing so by the time their youngest child was in first grade. Still, there are many women who do not wait even until their youngest child is old enough to attend nursery school before making the decision to migrate; 19 percent of them did so by the time the child was 1½ years old.

For women who have already begun working in Hanoi when they become pregnant, the pattern of when they return to work is more clear. These women are far less likely to wait until their child is old enough to attend school before they return to work; instead, they tend to resume working around the time that they stop nursing. More than 75 percent of women in this group said that they had returned to Hanoi within a year and a half of giving birth, and virtually all of them (98 percent) had returned to work before the child was old enough to attend nursery school.

It is tempting to think that women who start working in Hanoi (often for weeks at a time) once they stop nursing really do need the money, and for most of these women, this is undoubtedly true. A woman who returns to her village five months before her child is born and does not go back to work until the child is eighteen months old will have spent almost two years without any income from her street vending job. For most women, this is a long time. Still, no conclusions can be reached from this concerning women who wait longer or who do not even become roving street vendors until after they are finished having children. Most street vendors say that each village has very strict norms about when it is appropriate for a woman to leave a child at home so that she can go to

Huyen came to Hanoi for the first time in 1983, before *Doi Moi*...
She was unmarried at the time, and she was filled with a strong curiosity about the city and simply wanted to live there to experience what it was like. She joined a group of other women from her village in Hung Yen province who brought bananas into the city by train in order to sell them. She would leave her village at 2am, walk 10 km to the train station with 2 baskets of bananas, and arrive in Hanoi at 6am. She spent the night sleeping outdoors at the train station because there were no rooming houses for migrant street vendors at the time. She said that she was happy not to have to spend any money on lodging expenses, but she did live in constant fear of being arrested for vagrancy.

Huyen came to Hanoi this way four or five times over the course of the year, but she got married in 1984 and stopped coming. She stayed at home until the early 1990s when she resumed the job as soon as her third child stopped nursing at the age of 14 months. This time, she came to the city not out of curiosity but because she desperately needed the money. River barges had started going to and from a small port only 1km from her village, so she came to the city by boat instead of by train. She found that there were plenty of rooming houses for women like her, so she no longer had to spend the night outdoors. And because the rooming houses were near the Long Bien wholesale market, she no longer had to bring fruit from her village to sell.

Hanoi to work. They also say that they would be extremely reluctant, no matter how much they needed the money, to violate these norms. In some villages, it is considered acceptable to leave a child at home once the child has stopped nursing or after the child is two or three years old.

In other villages it is not, and it is customary instead for a woman to remain at home at least until the child can attend nursery school and very often until the child enters elementary school. The fact that more women are beginning to work as migrant street vendors even before they start having children, together with the fact that women who are already working in Hanoi when they become pregnant tend to return to work after they stop nursing, suggests that these norms are being tested in

> **Loan said that in her village in Phu Tho province...**
>
> it would be unthinkable for a woman, once she gave birth to a child to not stop working for 3-4 years in order to take care of that child. If she had another child after that, she would have to stop working for another 3-4 years. We asked her about street vendors from other villages and provinces who return to work as soon as they stop nursing their children. She said that this would be a matter of village custom and tradition but that in her village, it would be viewed in a very negative way.

many villages as rural living costs go up. Nonetheless, many women say that social norms continue to play an important role in shaping when a woman can either begin or resume working in Hanoi. They go on to say that there is a considerable amount of shame involved for women in their villages who find that they have no choice but to migrate sooner than is considered appropriate in those villages.

Migration, Child Rearing and Household Chores

Regardless of when a woman makes the decision to either start or resume her job as a roving street vendor following the birth of her children, she must factor into her decision the question of who will look after her children and perform other tasks associated with household reproduction while she is away. How she and her husband answer this question depends in part on whether the street vendor's husband also migrates in order to find work. For families in which the street vendor is the only one who migrates, much of the responsibility for taking care of the children while she is away falls on her husband. For families in which the husband also migrates, the task of taking care of the children clearly has to fall on someone else.

In fact, the options available to families in which both the husband and wife migrate are limited. It is rare for a woman to be able to entrust the care of her children for extended periods of time to anyone but close family relatives, and even within the network of family relatives, this task is most frequently undertaken by the husband's parents. This is part of the culture of gender in rural society whereby parents will typically take care of the children of their sons but, except in emergency situations and even then only for short periods of time, not the children of their daughters. This is true even a for a woman who has married someone from the same village and who has not

Tinh's daughters...

Tinh is a 30 year old basket lady whose husband now stays at home to look after their two daughters, aged 2 and 7. His parents are both deceased, and Tinh said that her own parents were too busy with their farm work and with taking care of their animals to help her out. If anything, she added, her parents would take care of her brothers' children and not hers. She then explained that it was the village custom for parents to take care of only their sons' children and not the children of their daughters. Daughters can ask their parents to help with their children but only in emergencies and only for short periods of time. At the end of our interview with her later on that day, we asked if, when her own daughters get married and have children, she will take care of them, and she quickly replied that of course she would. We then asked what she would do if she were to have a son who then had children when he got married. Here, she answered that she and her husband were too poor and that she didn't think that they could afford to have another child.

moved very far away from where her parents live. She may see them almost every day when she is at home, but she would rarely think of asking them to look after her children while she is working in Hanoi. In those cases where a woman can count on her own parents to help out, it is almost certainly because she does not have any brothers whose children also need to be looked after. The only other realistic alternative, finally, for a street vendor whose husband migrates at the same time, is for the children to take care of themselves. While this is not an option for women with very young children, it is not completely unheard of in families where the children are somewhat older.[77]

Partly for these reasons, in the vast majority of roving street vendor families the woman is the only one who migrates to find work. Of the 75 (out of 513) street vendors interviewed in 2006, 2008, and 2009, whose husbands also migrated, only 22 said that they and their husbands never were away from home at the same time. In the other 53 families, the street vendor and her husband were away at the same time at least occasionally. The median age of the youngest child in this latter group of families was six years, and in only one of them were there no school-aged children living at home. In most cases, the children were

---

When Nga's in-laws went against village norms...

In 2006, the brother of Nga's husband decided to leave their village to join his wife in Hanoi where she works as a street vendor and where he started to sell fruit from a bicycle. The two of them would spend at least 30 days at a time in Hanoi before one or both of them came home to look in on their two daughters, ages 9 and 4. Leaving children this young alone went against village norms, and while some people understood that the parents did this because they were poor and needed the money, most were highly critical of their decision.

While they were in Hanoi, care of the two children became the responsibility of Nga's family. At first, her own daughter, who was in 9th grade at the time, spent the night with them in their house. Nga was very upset about this because she was afraid that her daughter would spend her evenings playing with her two cousins instead of doing her homework. As a result, Nga's husband started spending the night at his brother's house while her daughter stayed home with her younger brother and her grandmother. Finally, once the grandmother, who was ill at the time, got a little better, she took over for Nga's husband. During the day, when they were not in school, the older child looked after her younger sister.

Nga remained worried about what her brother-in-law and his wife were doing and about how it would affect their children, so after the Tet holiday in 2007, she asked her husband to call a meeting of the entire family. It was here that she told the two of them that if anything happened with the children while they were in Hanoi, it would look bad not just for them but for the entire family. The family agreed that they would be allowed to continue working in Hanoi at the same time only for six more months and that after that, one of them would have to remain at home with the two children at all times.

left to the care of the husband's parents when both parents were away. The children were left to take care of themselves in 11 of the 17 families that could not count on help from the husband's parents; they were left to the care of the street vendor's parents and/or some other family member in only six of these families.

Whether his wife is the only one to migrate or she and he are away from home at different times, the husband frequently assumes much of the responsibility for providing care to the children while his wife is working in Hanoi. In 2006, when we asked 190 street vendors whose husbands either did not migrate or did not migrate at the same time as their wives who was generally responsible for the care and supervision of their children while they were in Hanoi, 57 percent responded that their husbands were. Another 12 percent said that their husbands and their husbands' parents shared general responsibility for their children while they were away, while one percent said that they shared this responsibility with one or more of their children. The husband's parents assumed this responsibility on their own in 21 percent of the responses.

In 2008, 2009, and 2010, we asked street vendors more specific questions about different child rearing and household tasks that were performed by their husbands. We also asked who else performed each of these tasks. The results are shown in Table 3.4, which includes the responses of 312 street vendors whose husbands either do not migrate or who never migrate at the same time as their wives.

Table 3.4: Tasks Performed While Street Vendor is in Hanoi

	Husband	Parents-in-law	Children	Other
at least some participation	88%	39%	69%	12%
look after children–daytime	69%	33%	16%	5%
look after children–evening	72%	27%	16%	3%
supervise homework	55%	22%	36%	5%
cook meals	60%	25%	40%	3%
wash dishes	33%	15%	62%	2%
go to market	60%	22%	30%	4%
clean house	48%	18%	52%	1%
wash clothes	51%	17%	49%	2%

312 families with children 18 or under: 2008-2010

Table 3.4 also shows the percentage of families in which husbands, husbands' parents, children, and others were involved in the performance of at least one of the listed chores.

One thing that stands out from this is that although 88 percent of street vendors said that their husbands participated at least somewhat in the performance of different child rearing and household chores, far fewer of their husbands were likely to participate, either alone or with the help of others, in the performance of any given chore. The highest incidences of husband participation are keeping an eye on the children during the day when they are not in school (69 percent) and in the evening (72 percent). Most other chores involve participation rates by men that are much lower. These are usually around 50 percent to 60 percent, but they fall even lower when it comes to washing dishes (33 percent) and cleaning the house (48 percent).

This means, and Table 3.4 also shows, that husbands are very often helped out while their wives are away, mostly by either their own parents or their children. A husband was able to rely on help from his parents in a total of 39 percent of the families, most often with watching the children during the day (33 percent) and with preparing meals and looking after the children after dinner (25 percent and 27 percent, respectively). Children helped out at least somewhat in 69 percent of the families. The highest incidences of children's participation are washing dishes (62 percent) and cleaning the house (52 percent), the two activities that husbands are least likely to engage in. Other people helped out in only 12 percent of families, most often by supervising the children's homework (five percent).

Table 3.5 shows a different way of looking at the help a husband receives for child rearing and household chores while his wife is in Hanoi. This table shows how many husbands perform each task by themselves, how many share responsibility for performing that task with others, and how many do not participate at all in the performance of that task.

Table 3.5: Tasks Performed by Husband While Street Vendor is in Hanoi

	Performs task alone	Shares task with others	Does not perform task
look after children–daytime	48%	21%	31%
look after children–evening	53%	20%	27%
supervise homework	46%	8%	45%
cook meals	34%	29%	37 %
wash dishes	22%	11%	67%
go to market	45%	14%	41%
clean house	30%	18%	52%
wash clothes	36%	16%	49%

312 families with children 18 or under: 2008-2010

Two things stand out from Table 3.5. First, when a husband performs any particular task, he is usually much more likely to perform that task by himself than he is to receive help in the form of others performing that task along with him. Preparing meals is the one exception to this. Here, the number of men who prepare meals on their own (34 percent) is slightly more than the number who share the task of cooking with others

(29 percent). For the remaining tasks, the number of men who perform a particular chore alone is significantly higher than the number who perform that chore along with others. The number of men who clean the house by themselves, for example, is 1.7 times higher than the number who share that task with others, and the number of men who wash dishes without any help is twice as high as the number who share that task.

The second, and perhaps more significant, thing that stands out from Table 3.5 is that for any given chore that needs to be performed when his wife is in Hanoi, that chore is very often not performed by the husband. For each chore other than looking after children during the day and at night, the husband does not perform the chore in at least 37 percent of street vendor families (in the case of cooking meals) and in as many as 67 percent of those families (in the case of washing dishes). We can conclude that the help a husband receives for any particular chore while his wife is in Hanoi is more likely to relieve him from performing that chore entirely than to involve someone else performing that chore along with him.

This last conclusion needs to be qualified somewhat by the fact, already noted, that husbands perform at least one of these chores in 88 percent of street vendor families. They perform at least two of them in 80 percent of families, three or more of them in 73 percent of families, and four or more in 62 percent of families. Thus, while the help that a husband receives while his wife is away often means that he does not have to assume responsibility for some child rearing and household chores, it rarely means that he does not have to assume responsibility for any of those chores. Traditional gender roles, consequently, appear to be somewhat (but not completely) reversed in most street vendor families, and many of the chores that a husband might typically expect to be performed by his wife are not automatically passed on to others when she is in Hanoi. This is a point to which we will return.

The nature of the help that a husband receives while his wife is away is particularly important in terms of the agricultural work that he must perform in cases where he is only a farmer and also in terms of allowing him leave home to work in cases where he has an outside job in addition

How Loan's children help out...

In 2007, Loan's older son was 13 years old and about to enter 9th grade, and her other son was 11 years old and about to enter 7th grade. Loan works in Hanoi anywhere from 15 to 30 days per month, and in order for her to do this, she and her husband rely heavily on the work their two sons do in terms of household and agricultural chores.

In the summer months, the two boys get up at 6am. Hoa, the older son, takes the family ducks and chickens out of the cage and feeds them. He then takes the chickens out to the family garden to peck around for food, while his younger brother, Hien, takes the ducks down to a local canal for a swim. If his father does not need the water buffalo to work in his fields, Hien brings it along with him so that it can graze along the banks of the canal. Hoa stays back in the compound to help his father feed the family pigs, after which he prepares enough slop to feed them for the rest of that day and the following morning. When this is done, he sweeps the house and the courtyard before heading out to the family rice fields where he picks spinach leaves, morning glory, and other plants that they grow along the edges of their fields to use in the pig slop. He returns to the house around 11am to prepare lunch, but if he has to help his father out in the rice fields, the younger son will come back to do this. After lunch, the two of them have two hours to play or rest as they choose, but by 3pm Hoa must return to the rice fields to pick more vegetable leaves, and Hien takes the ducks and water buffalo out for another walk. Hoa returns home a little early to wash the greens and puts them aside to use in making the pig slop the following morning. He then has to sweep the house and courtyard again. At 5pm, Hien comes home to start preparing dinner. The father also returns from the rice fields at this time, and he and Hoa feed the family pigs their third meal of the day. The three of them then bathe themselves at the family well. The ducks and chickens are put back in their cage at sundown, and the three of them then eat dinner.

Once school is in session, there is nobody to take care of the ducks, so Loan sells them to make some additional money. Hoa goes to school in the morning after feeding the chickens, so the younger son does all of the remaining chores except to prepare the pig slop. (He is still too young to do this, so Loan's husband does it after he returns from the fields at lunchtime.) Once the summer rice harvest is over, he is able to leave the water buffalo to graze on the fields by itself, and he comes back to sweep the house and courtyard and to prepare lunch. When he goes to school for the afternoon session, Hoa takes the water buffalo back out to graze while he cuts the plant leaves for the next day's pig slop. Hien prepares dinner after coming home from school, and the two brothers are then given one hour of homework time.

to farming. Because the typical street vendor is often away from her village for long stretches of time between planting and harvest seasons, much of the agricultural work falls on the husband, and because of this, he may need someone to help out around the house during the day. Similarly, if he is holding down an outside job, he may need to count on someone being able to prepare lunch and dinner and to perform various other household chores while he is at work.

The contribution that children make to the overall family economy by helping out their fathers with different household chores is something that needs to be emphasized.[78] It is common for children to know how to cook rice by the time they are seven or eight years old and to be able to cook an entire meal shortly after that. Young children are also expected to wash the dishes after each meal. In addition, they are frequently called upon to perform tasks that are not included in Tables 3.4 and 3.5. A street vendor family will rarely own a cow or water buffalo unless there is a child at home to graze it. The same is true for ducks, which need to be taken to water both in the morning and in the afternoon. Chickens require less work, but they still must be taken out of their cages and fed each morning before being turned loose in the family compound for the day. While husbands tend to do most of the work associated with raising pigs, children are often sent out to gather leaves or even to prepare the slop that pigs are fed each day. Many women tell us that it would be very difficult for them to continue as migrant street vendors and for their husbands to simultaneously continue as farmers without the contribution of their children to these other tasks.

Migration and Gender Roles

From our conversations with roving street vendors, we believe that the decision for a woman to become a migrant street vendor and for her husband to stay at home is in virtually all cases a family one in which the various reasons for her to go to Hanoi and for him to stay at home are discussed and ultimately agreed upon by both the street vendor and her husband. However this agreement is ultimately reached, we have shown that it must involve some understanding of who will perform different child rearing and household chores (chores that are typically performed by women) when she is away.[79] We have also shown that for most families, this agreement means that the husband will assume responsibility for some, but not all, of these chores. In other words, when a street vendor is working in Hanoi, there is a partial reversal of gender roles within her family. The question that we now turn to is whether this reversal is only temporary or whether circular migration contributes to a permanent transformation of traditional gender roles in the families of roving street vendors.

Because circular migration, by definition, means that street vendors go back and forth between Hanoi and the villages on multiple occasions over the course of the year, one way of looking at this question is to examine what happens when they are back in their villages. We show this in Table 3.6. It contains responses gathered in 2008, 2009, and 2010 from the same women who are included in Tables 3.4 and 3.5 above, and it can, consequently, be compared directly with those tables.

Table 3.6: Tasks Performed When Street Vendor is in Her Village

	Husband			Street Vendor		
	Performs task alone	Shares task with others	Does not perform task	Performs task alone	Shares task with others	Does not perform task
look after children–daytime	3%	29%	67%	50%	32%	18%
look after children–evening	4%	29%	67%	50%	32%	18%
supervise homework	12%	19%	69%	32%	22%	46%
cook meals	1%	12%	87%	73%	21%	5%
wash dishes	<1%	6%	94%	59%	15%	26%
go to market	2%	6%	92%	82%	11%	6%
clean house	1%	8%	91%	69%	19%	12%
wash clothes	1%	9%	90%	71%	19%	10%

312 families with children 18 or under: 2008-2010

Table 3.6 shows a dramatic fall in the percentage of families in which the husband helps out when his wife is back home. In terms of looking after the children and supervising them with their homework, the percentage

97

of families in which men do not perform these tasks is about 67 percent. For all other chores, the percentage is even higher, ranging from 87 percent of men who do not help out by cooking meals to 94 percent who do not wash dishes.

The decrease in the contribution by men to household and child rearing chores is most pronounced in terms of how many of them continue to perform any given chore by themselves once their wives return.[80] With the exception of looking after the children and helping them with their homework, however, the percentage of men sharing responsibility for these chores also drops. For tasks related to the supervision of children, many men wind up sharing responsibility with others, most often their wives.

Table 3.6 also shows that when they are at home, the burden of performing chores falls most heavily on women. Cooking meals, washing dishes, going to the market, cleaning the house, and washing clothes are all chores that in more than 50 percent of the cases women said they do by themselves. Looking after the children and supervising them with their homework are chores that they are less likely to perform alone, but their overall contribution to these chores is still high. Roughly 80 percent of them, either alone or with others, took on the responsibility of looking after the children both during the day and at night, and 54 percent assumed at least some responsibility for supervising them with their homework.

As noted above, most of the help that a street vendor receives for looking after the children and supervising them with their homework comes from her husband. For the other tasks, however, the help that she receives is more likely to come from either her children or her husband's parents than from her husband. Furthermore, when the street vendor is not involved in the performance of those tasks, her husband is much less likely to do them than are her children and, in many cases, her parents-in-law.

Another indication of how heavily the burden of caring for her children and performing other household chores falls back on women when they return home from Hanoi is in the total number of tasks they perform. Perhaps not surprisingly, virtually all street vendors (99 percent) say that they perform at least one of the chores listed in Table 3.6 when they are at home. Ninety-three percent of them perform four or more of those chores, and 77 percent say that they perform at least six of the eight chores listed. By contrast, 47 percent of husbands do not perform any of the chores at all. Only 11 percent perform four or more chores, while the number who perform six or more falls to five percent.

It seems clear, then, that whatever reversal in gender roles that takes place when street vendors are in Hanoi is only temporary, and the responsibility for child rearing and household chores reverts to them when they are back in their villages. The number of husbands who perform any of these chores alone is in most cases negligible, and with the exception of tasks involving the supervision of their children, the contribution they make by helping out with household chores is less than the contribution made by children or by the husband's parents.

Conclusion

We hope it is now clear that the extra income that basket ladies earn in Hanoi is essential for rural families, not only for their survival but also to enable their families to be better educated and housed. There are many social and cultural influences on the decision by a woman and her husband that she be the one to migrate, including village norms about the age at which a woman may leave her children. Our findings are similar to other case studies of rural circular migrants in Vietnam: most are not seeking permanent jobs in the cities, they follow patterns of migration that are heavily influenced by what other women in their villages do, and in Hanoi they usually live in guest houses with other women from the village or the commune.[81]

It appears that traditional gender roles do not constrain female circular migration, at least among the families of roving street vendors and junk dealers. However, this does not imply that gender roles have been reversed: our findings are similar to those of Resurreccion and Ha and Nguyen Binh,[82] which show that when women return to their villages, they also return to their household tasks. Husbands who did many of those tasks while their wives were away do, in some cases, continue to help out, but we find no evidence that circular migration has led to widespread changes in gender roles or in the traditional status of women vis a vis men.

Having shown how important the income earned in Hanoi is, we now turn to how roving street vendors actually earn it. It will become clear that living and conducting "business" in Hanoi are fraught with difficulties for basket ladies, and except for what they can earn, there is very little about their lives in the city that they find desirable.

CHAPTER 4

LIFE IN HANOI

During the time that a roving street vendor spends in Hanoi, much of her life is shaped by a network of social relationships that is rooted in the life and culture of her own village. These relationships provide an important source of support for her as she assumes the identity of a migrant woman working on her own in order to make money for her family back home. In significant ways, this social network helps make the work that she does in Hanoi easier for her. Still, very few roving street vendors find much that they enjoy about the work they do when they are in Hanoi. They live in crowded and noisy rooming houses that offer little more than a small space of flooring to sleep on. They get up early in the morning, often around 2 or 3am, in order to go to the market to buy their goods, and then they walk long distances with heavy loads that can reach 35kg or more. They are usually exhausted by the time they finish work and return to their rooming houses, sometimes late in the afternoon or early in the evening. They work in an almost constant state of fear of being stopped by the police, and they frequently have to deal with petty thieves, occasional scam artists, and other job-related risks. They do this work in a city whose people have, at best, mixed opinions about them and their presence there. While many of their customers are nice to them, street vendors know that they are generally viewed condescendingly, and even unkindly, as "country folk" or "peasants" and that they are considered to be subaltern members of Hanoi's society. Finally, and perhaps hardest of all for many of these women, scarcely a day goes by when they do not miss their children and wish they could be at home with them.

Village and Family Groups

Once a woman makes the decision to go to Hanoi to become a roving street vendor, she rarely goes entirely on her own. Instead, the typical street vendor comes to the city under the tutelage of another woman from her village, usually a member of her own extended family. This woman will teach her how to buy her goods and how to walk the streets of Hanoi in order to sell them. The street vendor will also take up lodging in the same rooming house as her tutor and will in this way become part of a much larger group of women who come from the same village or commune, some of whom are related to one another either by blood or by marriage and all of whom all live together while they are in Hanoi.

The group to which a roving street vendor belongs serves as a support network upon which she knows she can depend.[83] The group gives moral support and encouragement during the early difficult days when a street vendor is learning the job and away from her family for what is often the first time. Experienced street vendors also look to other members of their groups for moral support and encouragement during what can be long and difficult stays in Hanoi. Evenings tend to be when they miss family the most, especially on days when they have not made much money, and it would be much harder for them if they had to spend their evenings alone.

Members of a group frequently go to the market together in the mornings to buy their goods, and they help each other out with such things as carrying goods out of the market or watching the baskets and poles of those who are inside the market. Many of them sell in the same general area, and they often arrange to meet for lunch. They may also wait for each other at the end of the day before returning to their rooming house. In these ways, they are able to look after each other in case one of them runs into difficulty during the day. A street vendor can also depend on members of her group to help her out if she runs into problems with the police. Police harassment of roving street vendors throughout the city is common and often results in steep fines as well as the seizure of goods and equipment. A woman who has had her goods and equipment seized by the police will typically need to borrow money to cover the cost of new equipment and to purchase an inventory of goods to sell the next day. Under normal circumstances, it would be extremely difficult, if not impossible, for a woman to borrow this amount of money without returning home to her village, but because she can count on each member of her group to lend her a little bit, she is usually able to get back on her feet.

The village group plays another important role in shaping the life of a roving street vendor while she is in Hanoi. Although the group is structured largely on the basis of a social network that is rooted in village culture, it also offers a degree of freedom from that culture. In village culture, gender and kinship relations involve a complex set of codes of social conduct among individuals that affect the way those individuals see and interact with each other. In many ways, village women see each

Loi was the exception and came to Hanoi by herself...

When Loi made the decision in 1996 to start coming to Hanoi, she had no idea what she would do; she only knew that she needed money and had to find something. At the time, there were a few women from her commune who worked as basket ladies, but they were very competitive and refused to teach her the job. Instead, she found one woman who got her a job as a porter in the Long Bien market.

Carrying goods for other women who worked as basket ladies made her curious about the job, so after a while, she decided to teach herself. She did this by watching other women and trying to do exactly what they did. At first, she said, it was really hard. She had no idea about what goods to buy, about how to buy them, about how to sell them, or even about where to sell them. She didn't make very much money at first and even lost money on several occasions, but little by little, she was able to learn.

Loi told us this in 2009, adding that "By now, well I'd guess you'd have to say I'm pretty good at this job. After all, I've been at it for well over 10 years."

Loi also added that after teaching herself the job, she started to bring a number of her relatives and friends to Hanoi, and they are now part of the same group. They all get along very well, said one of these women. They look after each other, they don't steal from each other, and, after they all return to their boarding house at night, they have a good time together. "We really know how to laugh," she said.

other in terms of their relationships to men. Who her husband is, who her father or brother may be, and what the relative age of each of these men is within their own respective families all shape how other women are expected to interact with her and how she is expected to interact with them. When women are in Hanoi as part of a street vendor group, however, many of the expected codes of conduct are relaxed, and there is a tendency for women within the group to view and treat each other on a different, if not more equal footing. Some women say that the time they have together, especially in the evenings before they go to bed, affords them the opportunity to talk with each other about things that they might not talk about back in their villages and to form bonds with other women in ways that also would not be possible in their villages.

This does not automatically imply, however, that the changing ways in which women see themselves and each other as a result of the time that they spend together in Hanoi puts them in conflict with the traditional norms of village culture. Indeed, most women say that when they are back in their villages, they are too busy doing farm work, performing household chores, and watching their children to spend time with other women the way they do in Hanoi. Those social interactions in which they do engage typically take place on ceremonial occasions when the more traditional rules of behavior are in full force.

Long Bien Market

The Long Bien wholesale market, located on the bank of the Red River and very near to the center of town, is the preferred market for the majority of roving street vendors. In spite of earlier attempts on the part of the city to build newer markets on the outskirts of the city, Long Bien remains the most important market both in terms of the quantity and the variety of goods that are sold. In addition to its central location, the market is also important in the eyes of roving street vendors because of its close proximity to the many rooming houses that are located along the river and that provide lodging to a vast number of migrant workers in Hanoi's informal sector.

Most roving street vendors get to the Long Bien market by 3am. Those who get there much later than this say that the selection and quality of goods are greatly reduced. Once inside, they typically spend two to three hours before finishing their purchases. Although most of them have a fairly good idea of what fruits they will sell over the course of the year, they often make their final decision of what to buy, from whom to buy, and even how to buy only after they get to the market. The women rarely buy from the same wholesale merchant each day and instead spend a considerable amount of time visiting many merchant stalls to see what fruits are available on that day as well as to see what the different prices are. Price and availability of a good are often determining factors in the choice of what to buy, but other factors such as the success or failure of the previous day's sales enter into this decision as well. For example, if the profits from the previous day's selling were low or if it took too long into the previous afternoon or evening to finish selling all of her goods, a street vendor might decide to buy something different once she has seen what is available. Alternatively, if she found that the quality of the fruit on the previous day was not good, she might decide to buy a different fruit, or she might decide to pay a somewhat higher price for the same fruit by buying from a merchant who allows her to inspect the fruit rather than buying from a closed carton.

Once she makes her purchases, the street vendor must spend time cleaning and preparing the fruit. She does this outside of the market, often back at her rooming house. This work can take up to an hour or more and involves washing the fruit, throwing out any rotten pieces, and estimating the remaining weight in order to help determine the hoped-for selling price for the day. It also involves arranging the fruit on the baskets in what the she hopes is an appealing manner. Far from being a mundane task, the work involves deliberate strategies on the part of street vendors, some of which may involve a certain amount of cheating. For example, to render citrus fruit more tender and succulent, some women will strike the fruit on the ground several times to soften it up. Others do not hesitate to glue broken stems back onto pieces of fruit in order to make them more attractive. Asked about this, one woman blamed the customers themselves, saying that they insist on high quality fruit at a low price and that doing things like gluing fruit back together is often the only way to satisfy consumer demands.

Pricing Strategies

Typically, street vendors set a hoped-for per kilo price in their heads that represents a small markup over the purchase cost of their goods. They do this in the mornings after they have cleaned and prepared their goods but before setting out to sell them. Because they are expected to sell fruit for less than what people have to pay in shops or in the market, the desired markup is usually around VND1000 to VND2000 per kilogram above their purchase cost. Of course, this does not prevent them from occasionally trying to set even higher markups. Many of them use conversational techniques to judge the personality of a prospective customer in order to see if it might be worth asking for a higher price. They also try to do this on the 1st and 15th days of the lunar month and on other important lunar holidays because on these days people tend to buy more fruit than usual so that they can place it on their family altars as part of their ancestral offerings.

Having set the intended markup, they tend to be fairly rigid about their selling price in the early mornings even if it means losing a sale. On the other hand, bargaining is a common ritual throughout Vietnam, and most roving street vendors become increasingly willing to bargain with prospective customers as the day progresses. They know

Some basket ladies do cheat their customers...

Van told us of several "tricks" that some basket ladies use when they are selling their goods. These include placing a small magnet on their scales to make their goods appear to weigh more than they actually do. She spoke of one woman who told her that she tries to sell 0.8kg for the price of 1kg this way and that whenever she gets caught doing it, she feels as though she herself is the one who has been "robbed."

As for Hue, plums sold at the start of the season are the most profitable fruit she sells over the course of the year. She buys a better quality plum for VND15,000 per kilo and another, poorer quality plum of the same variety for VND8-12,000 a kilo. She mixes them together in roughly equal amounts and then sells the mix for VND3,000 per 100 grams. This way, she is able to make twice as much as what she pays for the more expensive plums. She says that her clients try to sort out the good plums from the others, but she keeps adding poorer quality plums to the mix.

what their break-even price each day is, and they usually wind up selling between the break-even price and the intended markup price. Only at the end of the day, especially if they are more tired than usual or if sales have been poor all day long, will some street vendors agree to sell whatever they have left at a loss. Even then, they will rarely agree to this if it means losing money for the entire day's work. Instead, they may decide to work a little bit longer or else bring home any unsold goods in the hopes that they will be able to sell them the following day for at least the break-even price.

After a street vendor and her customer agree on a price, there is also room for a certain amount of cheating when it comes time to weighing the purchased goods. Indeed, one of the most common customer complaints about basket ladies is that they cheat on the weight of the goods that they sell.[84] The scales they use are hand-held devices whose markings are not always legible, and even when the markings are easily discernible, the majority of their customers believe that street vendors can and often do cheat when weighing their goods.

While customers complain about their cheating, roving street vendors often find that they themselves have been the victims of cheating by the wholesale merchants from whom they buy their goods, and this too can affect their pricing strategies. A street vendor bases her markup on the purchase cost of the fruit she buys, but she knows that cost only after she cleans the fruit and after she throws out any spoiled or rotten food. The weight she buys also includes any ice that was put into the carton to keep the

Hoa is a 22 year old unmarried street vendor...
who gives all of the money she makes to her parents in order to help them pay off the money they borrowed to build a new house. She says that the wholesale merchants in the Long Bien market where she buys her fruit will only reluctantly let her bargain over the price. The problem for her is that she typically buys her fruit by the carton, and she is not allowed to inspect the quality of the fruit inside. The cartons weigh approximately 37kg, but the amount of bad fruit that she must throw out each day averages out to about 3kg. She then buys an additional amount of loose fruit so that she leaves the market with a total of 45kg of good fruit.

goods fresh. Since wholesale merchants frequently put more ice into the cartons than they say is there in order to increase their own profits, and since there is usually some spoiled or rotten fruit included in the cartons, the difference between the amount that a street vendor buys each day and the amount she can actually sell is often significant. While they generally try to account for this in their markup strategies, they must also pay attention to market forces so as not to set a price that nobody will pay. Indeed, almost all street vendors have experienced days when they lose money because they have been cheated by Long Bien wholesale merchants, and some of them say that they decide to not even bother going out on the streets if they know in advance that they will not be able to make any money on that day.

Selling Routes

Once a street vendor becomes familiar with a general section of Hanoi, she rarely leaves that area to sell in some other part of the city. Since the majority of women learn the job from other women from the same village and/or extended family, the decision of where to sell is usually made for them when they first arrive in Hanoi. A roving street vendor typically takes several days to learn how to get back and forth from where she is learning the job to her rooming house near Long Bien. It takes even longer to learn the various "tricks" of selling in that part of the city, so once she has mastered them she is usually reluctant to set out on her own to discover new parts of town.

Many street vendors sell in sections of the city that are located within a few kilometers of the Long Bien market, but others walk farther before they reach the places where they are used to selling. Some of them, especially those who have a long way to walk, do so with a few other members of the village group. Once they arrive, however, they almost always begin selling on their own. Many have selling routes that they like to follow, but these routes can vary from day to day. The precise route a street vendor takes on any given day depends on such factors as police presence, weather and traffic conditions, and the number of customers they find on any particular street. Indeed, street vendors often talk among themselves, with customers, and even with passers-by to find out which streets they should avoid and which streets are considered safe.

Regardless of the route a roving street vendor follows, it is not unusual for her to walk 10km or more before she finishes selling for the day. This is in addition to the distance she must walk to get to her selling area. Given the weights that they carry, this part of the job is exhausting, and they all know of streets and alleys where they can go at different times of the day to put down their baskets in order to sell or simply to rest. These spots include streets around the open-air markets that are located in virtually every part of the city. They also include sidewalk and alley spaces in front of shops or living quarters of people with whom they have developed an acquaintance. Basket ladies also know the hours when the police go home for lunch, and during these times they feel they can stop virtually anywhere in order to sell. Preferred lunchtime selling areas include spots in front of restaurants, office buildings, and schools. This is because most people in Hanoi are in the habit of eating fruit immediately after their meals, so selling in areas where there are large congregations of people who have just finished eating makes good business sense.

Risks While Selling

Roving street vendors face a number of risks that are associated with their job. These risks begin early in the morning as soon as they leave for the market. Long Bien market and its nearby streets and alleys are filled with petty thieves and drug addicts who know that the vendors must go to the market with relatively large sums of money in order to purchase their goods for the day. Street vendors often leave for the market with other women from their village group in order help each other fend off the aggressive behavior of those who loiter outside.

> **Thieves can be dangerous...**
> Hoa is a 20 year old, single street vendor who started coming to Hanoi at the age of 17. Her parents are too poor to pay the education fees for her two youngest brothers, so she pays for these with the money she makes in Hanoi. She frequently has goods stolen from her when she is out on the streets selling, but she has been warned by the other, older women in her group not to yell at the thieves for fear of being beaten. Still, when she does encounter a thief, she tries to explain to him that her goods have cost her a lot of money and then says "so please don't take too many."

Inside the market, the risks continue. It is extremely crowded at that time of day, and the women who enter are in almost constant pushing and shoving contact with others. There is little to prevent thieves from entering the market, and even though the street vendors try to keep their money well hidden, there is always the heightened risk of having it stolen when they are unable to pay close attention.

Another risk to roving street vendors comes from the Long Bien merchants themselves, and the words "mean", "aggressive", and "dishonest" are among those most commonly used by basket ladies to describe them. Virtually all of the merchants are believed to cheat on the weight of the goods sold. They often sell fruit in cartons that cannot be inspected, and street vendors frequently leave the market only to find that their cartons are filled with poor-quality fruit or excessive amounts of ice. Alarming numbers of women report having been beaten by wholesale merchants when they have tried to negotiate over the price of the goods, and even those who have not been beaten say that they know others who have been. The story of the roving street vendor who was supposedly beaten to death by a wholesale woman for arguing with her about the goods she was selling is another indication of the fear that street vendors have of Long Bien merchants. While we could not confirm this story (the woman was reportedly allowed to escape and was never prosecuted) it has become part of the lore of Long Bien, and the bad experiences that most street vendors have had with wholesale merchants makes it easy for them to believe it.

Once the women leave Long Bien and begin selling their goods, other risks arise. One constant concern is petty thieves who run off with small amounts of fruit when they think that a street vendor is not paying attention. Furthermore, because street vendors assume that most thieves are drug addicts or juvenile delinquents, they are often afraid of being attacked and robbed as they walk the streets and alleys trying to sell their goods. Theft also results from difficult customers who, often after lengthy bargaining, simply get up and leave without paying for the fruit they have taken. The amounts of fruit involved are generally small, ranging from whatever can be grabbed by hand to a plastic bag weighing perhaps a kilogram or less, but even this can put a dent in a vendor's daily profit.

Scam artists posing as customers pose another threat. By pretending to be very wealthy people who might make a large purchase, they try to lure a street vendor into a false sense of security and get her to let her guard down. One way to trick a street vendor into handing over a large amount of her own money is trying to pay with bills that require a lot of change. But the customer then takes back the large bill, saying they will actually pay with a smaller one. Having done

---

When Loi was tricked into turning over VND300,000 to a scam artist...

She was given a large bill for a purchase, but each time Loi tried to make change, the customer kept telling her to give her newer, cleaner bills instead. Because the woman did not haggle over the price, Loi was happy to have her as a client and did not mind changing the money for her. Also, because the woman was well-dressed, Loi did not think of her as a thief. Still, she is not sure how it was that she kept giving this woman money the way she did, and she is convinced that the scam artist put some kind of hypnotic drug on the first bill that she gave her. In any event, she has heard that other street vendors have been fooled in similar ways, and the women in her group have now decided to no longer sell to any well-dressed women on fancy motorbikes who try to pay with large bills.

---

that, the customer takes off with both the large bill and the large amount of change the street vendor initially offered. Although instances of this form of theft are significantly fewer than the theft of fruit by petty thieves and ornery customers, the amount of money involved is significantly higher and can result not only in the loss of a day's profit but also in the loss of a good portion of the capital needed to invest in the purchase of fruit each day.

Roving street vendors occasionally get into arguments over the space that they take up on the streets and sidewalks of the city. This is most likely to occur if they stop in front of storefronts or other buildings in order to make a sale. Many shopkeepers and building owners consider the space in front of their buildings as their "territory," so they try to chase away street vendors who stop there. Sometimes this happens quietly and without incident, but there are also times when the insults directed at a street vendor are met with a verbal response on her part. The resulting shouting matches can easily lead to pushing, shoving, and even beating in an attempt to chase the street vendor away. In addition to the verbal and physical abuse inflicted on the street vendor, she will usually lose a sale as a result of one of these incidents.

Another risk of bodily harm comes from the mounting volume of traffic on the streets of Hanoi. When this study first began to take shape in 1999, bicycles still constituted a significant proportion of traffic on the streets of Hanoi.[85] In a very short time, however, the number of motorcycles in the city exploded, and they quickly came to dominate the traffic patterns of the city. Now, motorcycles share the streets with an increasing number of cars and buses, and the traffic congestion in Hanoi has reached levels that were unimaginable only a few years ago. This means that crossing the streets in Hanoi can be downright dangerous. For roving street vendors, the most dangerous streets are those outside of Long Bien market because they must cross every morning with fully loaded baskets; many women have reported accidents there. However, traffic accidents occur throughout the city, and most street vendors either know personally or have heard of at least one accident involving a roving street vendor.

Problems with the Police

While all of the job-related risks described above mean that roving street vendors work with a certain amount of fear all day long, what they fear most is getting caught by the police. There are two principal regulations concerning the activities of roving street vendors. The first explicitly bans roving street vendors from certain streets of the city. These streets are usually clearly marked and tend to be located in and around the central part of town. The second regulation is much less clear both in terms of its meaning and in the way that it is enforced. This regulation effectively bans roving street vendors from sitting, standing, or stopping on any of the streets or sidewalks of the city. While this almost always means that it is illegal for them to sell from a fixed location, it is often interpreted to mean that they cannot sit, stand, or stop even temporarily in order to make a sale. In its strict interpretation, then, this regulation essentially means that while roving street vendors are free to walk along most streets of the city with things to sell, the act of actually selling any of those things puts them in violation of the law and subject to being stopped by the police.[86]

Enforcement of these rules typically results in a scene that is often aggressive, at times farcical, and almost always touched with an element of sadness for those who are caught. Local police officers work together with neighborhood officials who are identified by the red armbands they wear while on duty to enforce the regulations. The police will target streets in a neighborhood, and one or two of them will ride down those streets in a small truck with the neighborhood officials sitting on the back. One of the policemen usually carries a portable loudspeaker and repeatedly tells all "illegal occupants of the sidewalks" to leave the area immediately. Of course, by this time, word of the police raid has already spread far down the street, and most women are able to pick up their belongings and flee the area before they even see or hear the police. Unfortunately, there are usually a few women who are not able to get away in time, and when the police truck catches up with them, the neighborhood officials jump off and seize their goods and equipment. What follows is an often emotional scene in which the street vendors plead with the police to show them some mercy. The women know that there is virtually no possibility that they will be let off the hook completely, so they usually ask that their fine be kept to a minimum.

Policies concerning fines for street vending offenses have changed over the years. Earlier, fines were often levied on the spot, and the amounts paid were usually subject to negotiation, both in terms of amount and whether the vendor's goods would also be confiscated. Then, "Clean, Green, and Beautiful" tickets were instituted, and the per-ticket price was fixed at VND10,000 with anywhere from one to five tickets issued for each violation. Here, the only issue that was negotiable was how many tickets the vendor would receive. If she got hit with three or more, her goods would be confiscated, and she would have to go to a designated place to pay the fine before getting them back at the end of the day. If she could negotiate her way down to just one or even two tickets, she was able to pay the fine on the spot and continue on her way. More recently, the average fine has been VND150,000, but some pay even more while others are able to get away with less. Those who are lucky are able to either pay the fine or a bribe on the spot and walk away with all of their goods and equipment. The unlucky ones receive fines and have their goods confiscated. When this happens, their goods and equipment will be put on the back of the truck and carted off to the local police station. The street vendor must then walk to the station to receive a document that specifies her violation and the amount of the fine. She must then take that document to another government office to pay the fine and get a receipt, which she takes back to the ward police station to get her goods back. If the enforcement is particularly harsh, however, their goods will not be returned and their equipment will be destroyed. Meanwhile, back on the street, those who were able to flee the police will have long since returned to the spots where they were selling before the raid began.

The financial cost of getting stopped by the police is almost always significant and can frequently put a street vendor in dire straits. Even a relatively small fine eats into a portion or even all of her profits for the day. In the increasingly rare cases when she can pay the fine immediately and then continue selling as soon as the police are out of sight, the cost of getting stopped is limited to the amount of the fine. The effective cost in these cases, assuming that the fine itself is roughly equivalent to three day's profit (VND150,000), is in fact equal to the loss of four day's worth of income: three day's value for the fine, another day's value in lost profits for that day.

Of course, if a street vendor has her goods confiscated and they are not returned to her, or if they are returned to her too late in the day for her to be able to sell them, the purchase cost of those goods must also be added to the cost of getting stopped by the police. The impact of these lost inventory costs can be significant. Generally speaking, fruits with a higher per kilogram purchase price involve a higher inventory cost, while fruits with a lower unit purchase price involve lower inventory costs. Given the weights that most street vendors carry, the daily inventory costs typically are about VND250,000. Inventory costs rarely fall much below VND150,000, and for some goods, such as oranges, they can be as high as VND500,000. Assuming a daily profit of VND50,000, a VND250,000 inventory loss as a result of getting stopped by the police can mean the loss of five day's worth of income. Even a VND150,000 inventory loss would take at least three days to make up, and a VND500,000 inventory loss could take up to two weeks to recover. If the street vendor's pole and baskets are also seized, the cost in each case would increase by approximately another day's income. It is little wonder, then, that most street vendors become as depressed as they do after the police seize their goods and equipment and why many of them say that it can take several days or more before they build up the courage to go back out on the streets.

Street vendors say that police harassment is a daily fact of life for them and that they are always afraid of getting stopped. At the same time, the frequency and intensity with which the regulations concerning street vending activities are enforced varies and is often the result of decisions taken at high levels of municipal government. In its role as the capital city of Vietnam, Hanoi is frequently the site of international conferences, sporting events, diplomatic visits, and other events that are seen as important to building the city's image as a modern, international city. The presence of women walking around the city with baskets and poles during these events strikes some as undermining that image.[87] In the months leading up to these events, consequently, the police are likely to begin a crackdown on roving street vendors, and the chances of getting caught by the police during a crackdown increase dramatically. Each crackdown, in turn, becomes increasingly severe as the date of the event approaches.

The most significant police crackdown in the last decade was in the ten-month period leading up to the South East Asia (SEA) Games, which took place in December, 2003. As the crackdown got worse, virtually all fines resulted in the seizure of goods and equipment, and most street vendors felt far more in jeopardy from the police than they ever had before. Many left the city entirely, and the rest cut back on both the number of days that they stayed in Hanoi and the number of hours per day that they worked in order to reduce the risk of being caught by the police.[88]

The most trouble Loi ever had with the police...

was during the crackdown leading up to the 2003 SEA Games. She is not sure how many times she was stopped, but she does remember that the police seized all of her goods and then fined her eight times during that period. The worst stretch was when she got stopped five times in a row. The first time, the bicycle she had started using to bring her goods down to where she sells broke down just as the police were driving by, so they stopped and took her and all of her goods to the station. The other women in her group knew they hadn't seen her all day, and when they got home and found that she wasn't there, they figured she had been stopped and went down to the police station to find her. Loi had just come back from her village and didn't have much money, so they paid her fine. The police decided to let her keep her goods this time, but they wouldn't let her go until after dark. The next day she was carrying some oranges into a café that she sells to, and the police got her again. She begged them to let her keep her goods, but they wouldn't listen so she just sat there and cried. When they found out about it, the women in her group lent her VND500,000 so that she could buy more oranges the next morning. After she lost everything again the next day, they all decided that she should go back to her village to "get rid of her bad karma." She stayed home for two whole days, but when she came back to Hanoi she was stopped twice more. The police confiscated everything from her both times. The first time they wouldn't even let her speak, but the next day she says that they at least let her plead her case before throwing everything in the back of their truck and driving off.

Once the event that has caused a police crackdown is over, the crackdown tends to diminish in intensity, and most street vendors eventually feel as though they can resume work as usual, at least until the next crackdown. In early 2008, for example, the city announced a new policy about enforcing rules against street vending of all types, including fixed and roving sellers. By July of that year, the city had listed 62 streets on which street vending would be prohibited. One effect of the new policy was that in 2009, when we asked basket ladies about it, 47 percent of those we spoke to said that the ban on vending on major streets had caused them to work less than they had before. In addition, sixty-seven percent said that the ban had caused their income to fall, and many added that police pressure was making the job harder, not simply because of the fines and confiscations, but also because they had to seek out smaller streets on which to sell or move around more in order to avoid the police. While the ban was strictly enforced soon after its implementation, more recent enforcement appears to be much more lax. Nevertheless, this is the most recent example of the tide turning against roving street vendors.

Living Conditions in Hanoi

Because roving street vendors come to Hanoi to work to make money to help their rural families survive, it is not surprising that they live what can best be described as frugal lives while they are in the city. As we discussed in the previous chapter, many feel that they are much better at saving money and not spending it on themselves than their husbands are. While most street vendors express confidence in their own husbands, they share a widespread perception that men in general are far more likely to spend the money they make on cigarettes, gambling, alcohol, and various forms of licentious behavior. They believe that women are better able to think of the needs of their families and, consequently, better able to save money instead of spending it on themselves.

Consequently, roving street vendors live in austere conditions while they are in Hanoi. Most of them sleep in rooming houses that are within walking distance of the Long Bien market. The houses are two or three stories high and are located between the bank of the Red River and the dike road that runs along the river for the length of the city. The entire area is prone to flooding during the monsoon season, and some street vendors report having had to use small boats on occasion to go to and from work. The landlord and his or her family typically live on one floor of the house and rent the rooms on the other floors to street vendors and other migrant workers in Hanoi's informal sector. The rooming houses tend to be very crowded, and there is an almost total lack of privacy for the people who live in them. In 2007, for example, we found that the median number of people sharing a room was 10, but having 20 people in a single room was just as likely as having 5 to a room. Everyone sleeps on the floor, and they need to make room for the few personal belongings the women have brought to Hanoi. Some landlords provide mosquito nets in the summer and blankets in the winter, but many women say that they have to provide their own if they want to use them. The same is true for the straw mats that they sleep on.

The majority of street vendors have free use of utilities in their rooming houses, but there are some landlords who control the use of electricity and water. The heat and humidity in Hanoi can be oppressive, and while almost all rooms have a fan in them, 20 percent of the 205 women we asked in 2007 said that they were only allowed to turn it on at certain times of the day. This is usually around 7pm, and those who return home earlier must wait before they can use the fan. Most of the women eat their meals in street food restaurants, but those who wish to cook dinner at home have to pay an additional charge each day for the use of an electric rice cooker.

Water tends to be less strictly controlled than electricity, but in houses where it is controlled, street vendors say that life can be difficult. Some of the rooming houses near Long Bien still have unmetered water, and in these houses street vendors can use as much water as they like. In houses where there is metered running water, however, landlords sometimes impose strict limits on how much water each tenant is allowed to use. In these houses, each tenant usually has a small pail of water for bathing and another small pail for washing her clothes. Each pail contains about a gallon of water, and some women say that this is barely enough to wash and rinse themselves, much less their articles of clothing. In 2007, five percent of the women we interviewed said that they did not have enough water to bathe.

When we asked about restrictions on using the toilet, seven percent of the women said that they did not have any access at all to an indoor toilet. In these cases, women who cannot wait to use a public toilet in the morning are forced to use plastic bags, which they then dispose of when they leave the house to go the market. In the remaining cases, use of the toilet was largely unrestricted, but there are still a number of instances where it is not. The typical toilet in the Long Bien rooming houses is a "squat" toilet, flushed either by opening and closing a valve on the water feed pipe or by dipping water from a nearby pail and pouring it into the toilet. Either way, it would be easy for a landlord to monitor water usage, and some of them do in an attempt to limit it. Also, a few street vendors said they had to pay a fee each time they used the toilet, and another woman said that it was only available until 9pm.

Hue stayed in a rooming house with 19 other women from her village...

They all shared a single room with another group of street vendors from Thai Binh and Nam Dinh provinces, and the total number of people living there at one time could reach as high as 35 people. In 2005, the women in Hue's group decided to move to a new rooming house, but what they didn't know about the new place before they moved in were the landlady's three house rules. First, a fixed amount of water was put out each day, and the women who stayed there were not allowed to have more than this. Each person was given a plastic pail containing 5 liters for bathing and two small bowls of water for washing their clothes. Hue says that they need more than this to get their clothes clean, and they often try to steal a third bowl when the landlady isn't looking. Second, the fan in the room is only allowed to be turned on at night. If Hue returns home early, she will try to turn the fan on when it is hot, but she almost always gets caught and has to turn it back off right away. Third, the women who stay there are only allowed to use the toilet to urinate. Hue says the landlady sleeps in a room next to the toilet and listens to how much water is used to flush it. She can tell from this whether or not a anyone has broken her toilet rule, so Hue and the other women in her group must all wait until they get out on the streets each morning to use a public toilet.

Van couldn't take it either...

Van and her sisters lived together while they were working in Hanoi, and they changed rooming houses twice before finding one that they liked. The first was too crowded, and in order to make even more room to rent out, the landlord made many of the women sleep on a raised platform with not even enough room to sit, much less stand. Van said that they were living like "pigs in a cage." They moved to another house, but there they were always getting yelled at by the landlord's family. The other tenants worked as sidewalk barbers and sellers in shops, so they did not have to get up in the middle of the night to go to the market. Because Van and her sisters were the only ones who did, the landlord's wife was constantly complaining to them about having to wake up in order to let them out of the house each morning. Then, when they got home at the end of the day, they had to deal with the landlord's mother who never gave them enough water but yelled at them anyway for using too much. They decided that they couldn't take the complaining and yelling any longer, and they finally found a third house where the room that they sleep in was much larger and where they could use as much water as they want.

The quality of meals that roving street vendors eat while they are in Hanoi is not much different from the housing conditions in which they live. In an effort to keep their living costs down, some of them (10 percent in 2007) skip breakfast entirely. The rest usually eat a bowl of rice noodle soup that they purchase in one of the many street restaurants found near where they live. This relatively skimpy breakfast leaves many of them hungry, and in our 2007 survey, one-third of the women who ate breakfast said that they were hungry once they got out on the streets and started to sell. Lunch and dinner meals each typically consist of three basic dishes: a bowl of rice, a serving of leafy green broth, and a main plate served with either salt, soy sauce, or fish sauce. The main plate sometimes consists of meat, fish, or poultry, but it can also be simply an egg or some tofu.

Most roving street vendors do not finish working before lunch, so they have to eat this meal in one of the many street food restaurants that are scattered throughout the city. These restaurants have also become popular lunchtime spots for office workers, and some street vendors feel that the relatively high office worker incomes have caused the price of street food to go up beyond what they can afford. As a result, many basket ladies order smaller portions of food for lunch, and this often leaves them hungry. When asked about this in 2007, 18 percent of street vendors said that they were usually hungry after eating lunch. By contrast, the restaurants near Long Bien where those women who do not cook for themselves eat dinner are frequented almost entirely by migrant informal sector workers like themselves, and for the same amount of money they are generally able to get larger servings of food. If they spend a little more money for dinner than for lunch, which many of them do, it is usually because they are just plain hungry at the end of each day. They may also buy a cup of tea to drink after dinner, but buying something to drink during the day while they are on the job is generally considered a luxury. Instead, most street vendors try to find a sympathetic shopkeeper or building resident who is willing to give them a glass of water when they get thirsty.

Income Earned as a Roving Street Vendor

As we have already shown in this chapter, the amount of money that a roving street vendor is able to make each day depends on a number of factors. It depends on the quality and purchase price of the goods that she buys each morning when she goes to the market. It also depends on her pricing strategy and on how successful she is in realizing that strategy over the course of the day. It depends, finally, on other things, such as how lucky she has been in avoiding the police, how tired she feels, how hot it is, or whether it is raining heavily. For most street vendors, this means that there is a significant variation in the amount of money that they make from one day to the next. In fact, most of them do not really know how much money they have made until they return to their rooming houses at the end of the day and are able to actually count it. Once she counts it, a street vendor typically puts aside enough to cover the purchase cost of her goods the next morning. She also takes out enough money to pay her rent for the night as well as enough for her meals and other living expenses the next day. The rest represents her take-home income for the day and is either entrusted to the landlord for safekeeping or, in cases where she does not trust the landlord, carried with her at all times.

A street vendor's annual take-home income, in turn, depends on how many days she works in Hanoi over the course of a year. In Chapter 2, we showed that this is a function of how she responds to the numerous and at times conflicting demands that are placed upon her time. In Chapter 3, we looked at the take-home income of roving street vendors for 1999 and 2002, and we analyzed the importance of this income in terms of national poverty thresholds and in terms of the national distribution of consumption and income. In that chapter, we saw that the amount money that a typical circular migrant street vendor in 1999 was able to put aside as take-home income at the end of each work day was VND10,500. The average number of days that she worked was 191, meaning that her annual take-home income was VND2,005,500 and that her annualized daily take-home income was VND5500. We also saw that by 2002, the take-home income of a typical street vendor had gone up to VND14,500 per day. The total number of days that she worked that year had also gone up to 216, and her annualized daily income had gone up to VND8500.

Table 4.1: Street Vendor Take-home Income

Year	Days Worked	Daily Profit	Take-home Income per Work Day	Annual Take-home Income	Annualized Daily Take-home Income
1999	191	VND 17,500	VND 10,500	VND 2,005,500	VND 5500
2002	216	VND 23,000	VND 14,500	VND 3,132,000	VND 8500

(Numbers have been rounded to nearest VND500)

Table 4.1 has the same data as Table 3.1 in Chapter 3, but it also includes a street vendor's daily profit, which is what a street vendor is able to make after paying the purchase cost of her goods each day but before paying her daily living expenses. This amounted to VND17,500 in 1999 and VND23,000 in 2002. In Table 4.1, as in Table 3.1, we see that annualized daily income for a typical street vendor increased by 56 percent from 1999 to 2002. This increase was the result of an increase in her take-home income per work day of VND4000 and an increase of 25 days in the amount of time she spent working in Hanoi. Annualized daily income is the amount of money calculated on a daily basis that is available to a street vendor and her family to help cover the types of village expenses that were discussed in Chapter 2. As we also discussed in Chapter 3, the amount of money that a street vendor is able to make each day has continued to increase, but what we argue below is that making money from this job has become much more difficult than it was in the past.

Looking first at the increase in take-home incomes, we found that by 2006, in a survey of 233 circular migrant street vendors of child-bearing age, the median take-home income per work day had increased to VND20,000, a 38 percent increase over what it was in 2002. In 2007, we found that for many women this figure had increased to between VND25,000 to VND30,000, and by 2010 it was almost VND35,000.

Because we do not have any systematic data on how many days per year the typical street vendor worked in 2006, 2007, or 2010, we cannot estimate the median take-home income on an annual or annualized daily basis. Still, we can provide a range of take-home incomes for those years calculated on the basis of different numbers of days worked. We show this in Table 4.2, where we assume the take-home incomes per work day discussed above: VND20,000 in 2006 and just under VND35,000 in 2010.

The days of work figures in Table 4.2 are for illustrative purposes only. The figure of 180 days represents an average of 15 days per month, or approximately half of the year spent working in Hanoi. We chose the figure of 216 days per year because it represents the average number of days worked in 2002. The annual and annualized daily income amounts corresponding to this figure, consequently, allow us to look at what would have happened to a street vendor's income in 2006 and 2010 if she worked the same number of days as she did in 2002. Finally, the figure of 240 work days per year represents an average of 20 days per month spent in Hanoi. We use this figure because most basket ladies point to the sharp increases in virtually all of their village living expenses over what they were at the beginning of the decade.

Because of the impact of inflation on their living costs, it is reasonable to assume that many basket ladies were spending even more time working in Hanoi than they were in 2002. However, as long as a street vendor continues to work as a circular migrant, balancing the need for cash against the many reasons she needs to be at home, it would also be fair to assume that there is some limit to the amount of time that she could spend in Hanoi. We have already shown in Chapter 2 that there are at least some months of the year when it is simply not possible to spend 20 days working in Hanoi, meaning that she would have to spend far more than 20 days in Hanoi in other months in order to work a total of 240 days. From our interviews, we know that circumstances force some street vendors to work more than 240 days per year, but it would be difficult for the vast majority of them to do that. For example, we know that many street vendors work 25-30 days in some months, but that is a pace that they cannot, for reasons we discussed in Chapter 2, sustain over an entire year.

Table 4.2: Effect of Days Worked on Street Vendor Take-home Incomes: 2006-10

Year	Take-home Income per Work Day	Days Worked	Annual Take-home Income	Annualized Daily Take-home Income
2006	VND 20,000	180	VND 3,600,000	VND 10,000
		216	VND 4,320,000	VND 12,000
		240	VND 4,800,000	VND 13,000
2010	VND 34,900	180	VND 6,282,000	VND 17,000
		216	VND 7,538,000	VND 20,500
		240	VND 8,376,000	VND 23,000

(Annualized daily take-home incomes have been rounded to nearest VND500)

Clearly, street vendors in 2006 and 2010 who worked fewer than 180 or more than 240 days in Hanoi would have had annual and annualized daily incomes that fall outside of the ranges included in Table 4.2. What is also clear is how important both daily take-home income and the number of days worked per year are to annual take-home income. For example, a basket lady who worked 180 days in 2006 could have increased her annual take-home income by 133 percent if she worked 240 days in 2010: her daily take-home income had increased by 75 percent, and she worked 33 percent more days.

In addition to these pressures, while we lack data for 2012, we do know that living costs in Hanoi have gone up dramatically since we began our study. In 2000, the typical roving street vendor spent VND5000 per day on meals, and in 2003, she spent VND6000 per day.[89] By 2007, however, it was not unusual for a street vendor to spend VND15,000 per day on meals alone and slightly more than this if she bought something to drink during the day while she was working. The increase in lodging costs has also been significant. It cost VND2000 per night in 2000 to stay in a rooming house and VND2500 per night in 2003. By 2007, the cost of spending the night in Hanoi had gone up to at least VND4000, and more than half of the 100 women asked about lodging costs said that they had to pay VND5000 per night. In addition, many landlords had begun to charge a monthly rent of VND150,000. Because most migrant street vendors do not spend an entire month in Hanoi, the cost per night spent in Hanoi for women who were forced to pay a monthly rent would have been even higher than VND5000. By 2011, monthly lodging costs for many women had risen to VND300,000 and above.

Any increase in daily living expenses has a direct impact on how much money a street vendor is able to put aside each day, so it should be clear that the only way her take-home income can go up is for her profit to also rise. To illustrate this, first consider a street vendor who in 2002 made a daily profit of VND23,000. Since her living expenses were VND8500, her take-home income as shown in Table 4.1 was VND14,500. Now consider a street vendor in 2010 whose take-home income had gone up to VND34,900. Given that her daily living expenses had gone up to at least VND20,000 (the figure from 2007), her profit would have had to have been approximately VND55,000.

In order for a street vendor to see her profit go up, however, she would clearly have to change one or more of the ways in which she does business. For example, she could change her pricing strategy and try for a higher markup. However, because street vendors are almost always forced to lower their price over the course of the day, that strategy would be hard to accomplish. As a consequence, they would also have needed to carry more weight than they did in the past in order to obtain a higher profit. For instance, a street vendor who carried 25 kg of goods with a markup strategy of VND1500 in 2002 would have had a difficult time making a profit of VND45,000 to VND50,000 by relying only on a higher markup of VND2000. Instead, she would have been more likely to try for the higher markup while at the same time carrying, say, 30 kg. Carrying more weight, in turn, would generally mean having to spend more time each day selling, especially since a street vendor in 2010 was confronting both more competition on the supply side and changing buying habits of customers on the demand side. We can see, therefore, that the things a street vendor must do in order to increase her profit (try to charge a higher price, carry more weight, and work longer hours) and thereby earn more take-home income simultaneously make the job of selling more difficult.

Conclusion

In the very early morning, vendors go to buy goods in Long Bien market where they are frequently cheated and demeaned. Then, they spend the day walking many kilometers with heavy loads during which they risk being cheated by customers, robbed by drug addicts, hit by motorbikes, or, worst of all, caught by the police who fine them and/or confiscate their goods. At the end of the day, they return to crowded rooming houses where they lack privacy to sleep before they begin the cycle again the next day. In order to increase the amount of money they are able to take home to their families, street vendors take measures to reduce the costs of their living in Hanoi: many do not eat breakfast, and even when they do eat breakfast and increasingly expensive lunches, too many are left hungry afterwards.

For a street vendor from the countryside, life in Hanoi brings with it few advantages, no luxuries, and long, arduous days of walking and selling. Vendors find most comforting the fact that they are able to live and sometimes work with women from their villages or their communes. Sharing housing allows vendors to share experiences and provide mutual support during their stays in Hanoi. Set against whatever comforts come from living with and sharing experiences with people from their villages is the constant pain of missing their families, especially their children.

This picture of street vendor life in Hanoi might prompt one to wonder if it is worth it for them to put up with so much. That so many women have worked at this job for many years, and that others continue to follow in their footsteps, leaves little doubt that street vendors are being truthful when they tell us, as they do repeatedly, that their families really need the money and there is nothing else for them to do to get it.

Van listed for us what she saw as the advantages and disadvantages that Hanoi and her village both offered...

Hanoi	Village
Large selection of food. Can find almost anything.	Market is 3km away. Selection of food is limited and quality often not good.
More comforts, especially running water and electricity.	Electricity not stable, can't run a refrigerator. Water comes from traditional wells and only enough for 9 months. 15-30 days each year when no water, and 2 months when usage must be curtailed.
Everyone looks after themselves. No sense of other. No sense of community.	Things can be left outside and nobody will steal them.
Don't have to worry about being the subject of rumors and gossip.	Always at risk of being the victim of unfounded rumors.
Hanoi is where I can make a living.	My village is where I want to live.

CHAPTER 5

CONCLUSION

We have enjoyed being witnesses to Vietnam's dramatic successes in economic development over the past decade or so. During that time, we have come to know a group of women that has benefitted greatly from the policy of renovation (*Doi Moi*) and the growth that has resulted from it. Through patterns of circular migration, these women have worked as roving street vendors in the informal sector of Hanoi's economy in a way that has allowed them and their families to maintain their rural identities. As we look to the future, however, we see a number of factors that may well threaten the nature of this job, a job that has been the way out of poverty for a significant number of rural women and their families. We conclude this book by looking at some of these factors, many of which can be looked at in terms of changing demand and supply conditions for the goods that roving street vendors sell.

On the demand side, the city has changed dramatically since our study began, and consumers have many more options of where to buy food than in even the recent past. There has been a proliferation of increasingly popular supermarkets throughout the city. Open-air markets are numerous, and the city has initiated a campaign to renovate many of them in order to make them more attractive. The number of stationary sellers, particularly those selling from makeshift shelves put up alongside major arteries in parts of the city, has also increased. Street vendors have also pointed to the growing number of upscale cafes at which office workers, instead of buying fruit from a street vendor, now go to consume fruit juices and fruit cocktails. Increasingly crowded streets are another deterrent to buying from basket ladies because the traffic, especially cars, makes it hard for motorbike-riding customers to stop and buy.

The growing number of options that food buyers now have means that consumer attitudes toward street vendors are likely to have an increasingly important influence on how much money these women are able to make from the job. When we conducted a survey in 2012 of 270 food buyers, we found strong and divided opinions about the presence of roving street vendors in the city and about the food they sell.[90] The good news for street vendors was that 67 percent of those respondents with an opinion did not support banning street vendors entirely. This compares to 51 percent who did support a ban when we conducted a similar survey in 2004.[91] The most common reasons given in 2012 for not supporting a ban were that street vendors need the income (30 percent) and that they provide convenient sources of food (11 percent). An additional 9 percent said that street vendors were an important part of the culture of Hanoi. On the other side of this question, 11 percent of the respondents said that street vendors should be banned because they make traffic worse, 10 percent because of the poor quality of the food that they sell, and another 10 percent saying that they made the city look bad.

In terms of buying practices, the news for roving street vendors is also quite mixed: 30 percent of respondents do not even buy from them, compared to only 11 percent who do not patronize supermarkets, and the 1 person who said she did not use traditional markets. The good news is that 65 percent of respondents said they had not changed the frequency with which they buy from street vendors over the three-year period prior to the 2012 survey, while the bad news is that 30 percent said that they had either stopped buying from or had cut back on the frequency that they buy from street vendors. Additional bad news comes from the 50 percent of respondents who said that they buy from supermarkets more frequently now than they did before and the 35 percent who said that they buy more from open-air markets.

Another factor that might work against roving street vendors in the future is that as incomes of Hanoi residents continue to rise, there will likely be a move away from buying from them. In Chapter 4, we discussed the problems that confront street vendors as they are expected to sell good-quality fruits and vegetables at a low price. Not surprisingly, people with low incomes figured prominently among those in our 2012 survey who favored buying from street vendors. Another group (27 percent) pointed to the generally poor quality of the goods sold by street vendors. Consequently, assuming incomes continue to rise over the coming years, it may be that concerns about quality take precedence over concerns about price.

Supply-side pressures on roving street vendors are equally important. The increase in the number of women coming to Hanoi to work as roving streets vendors is by far the most commonly cited reason for why it is more difficult to make money from this job. Some women substantiate this claim by pointing to the number of women from their villages who have recently taken up this job, others point to the fact that their rooming houses are more crowded, and still others simply point to the number of women buying fruit each morning in the Long Bien market. Their claim is that not only has the increase in the number of sellers hurt in terms of more competition out on the streets, but it has also become more difficult to find good-quality fruit to buy each morning.

We tend to believe street vendors who complain about these supply side pressures, and we see no reason to believe, at least in the near future, that these pressures will taper off. As we discussed in Chapter 2, as more and more young women who did not receive any land use rights under the 1993 distribution get married and start to raise families of their own, land pressures may intensify. Many of these women, especially those who did not finish high school, will likely face an even greater need to migrate than did women of their parents' generation.

In Chapter 4, we argued that street vendors' incomes are higher now than they have been in the past, but we also argued that it is significantly harder now to earn those incomes. The changing demand and supply conditions that we have discussed above and that we expect to continue will, again, not make it any easier to earn an income from this job. While we bemoan the effects that these changes are having and will continue to have on the lives of basket ladies, we also understand the powerful effects that modernity and economic growth both offer and impose on all Vietnamese. The clock will not be turned back to those times when street vendors believe it was easier to earn income.

At the same time, we argue strongly against continued policy measures on the part of city officials to curb or even eliminate the street vending activities that have been so important to so many women and their families. It is a common refrain among street vendors, when asked why they took up this occupation, to say that there was nothing else for them to do. They answer similarly when asked about what they would do if they could no longer work as street vendors. With their low education levels and lack of training for formal sector work, they believe, probably correctly, that farming and animal husbandry, plus this type of selling, are the only types of jobs they are suited for. When pushed to speculate about what they would do if they could not do this work, many say that they would try to do more intensively what they already do at home: raise more animals or try to cultivate more land. However, these are the options they and their families have long had, so the prospect of returning to their villages to help farm more intensively is not really among the viable options open to street vendors who wish to improve their standard of living.

We believe that the wrong policy measures now would be those intended to undermine the way the informal sector works.[92] Instead, policy formulation should operate with an explicit recognition that the informal sector in Vietnam (as elsewhere) has played and will continue to play a pivotal role in the country's development.[93]

We believe that one of the reasons the *Doi Moi* reforms were as successful as they were was because they were internally generated and not imposed from the outside. This allowed the government to deal with important issues of timing and sequencing of policy decisions differently. The government dealt with these issues in a somewhat flexible manner and in terms of its own priorities, one of which was to ensure that everyone benefited from those reforms. We also believe that another reason the early reforms were as successful as they were was because they were "organic," meaning that they came out of actions that ordinary people and organizations were already taking to ameliorate the effects of central planning and collective farming.[94] In implementing its reforms, the government incorporated and legalized much of what was already happening.

We wonder why a similarly enlightened approach would not work in the case of roving street vendors. It is our belief that in the future, Hanoi's informal sector will likely look very different from what it is today, but we also believe that it will continue play the same role in helping individuals and families who either cannot or do not want to work in the formal sector improve their living conditions. In terms of the roving street vendors studied in this book, we believe that the demand and supply-side pressures discussed above—the growth of a larger urban middle class, more modern food-buying options, more cars in the streets, more competition among street vendors themselves—will not take too long a time to yield the outcome seemingly so desired by city officials in Hanoi: fewer and fewer roving street vendors. Even without government action to curtail street vending activities, customers will turn to more modern options, as they have been doing in greater and greater numbers already, and street vendors will find it increasingly difficult to make their profits and so be forced into other jobs or to sell in other places and in other ways. We suggest letting change happen at its own pace and that the government focus instead on efforts to improve and expand the prospects of informal sector job seekers so that some of those displaced by the forces of development, and certainly their descendants, will have other income-earning options.

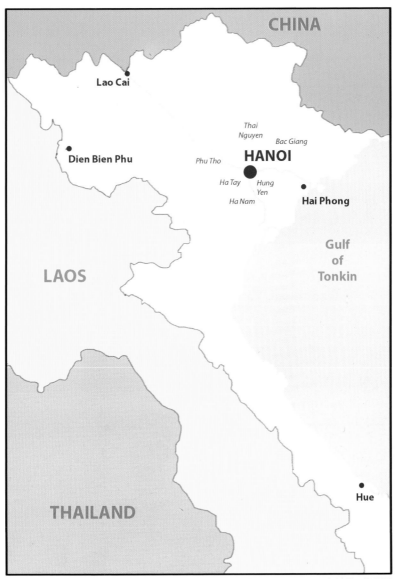

CHINA

Lao Cai

Thai
Nguyen
Bac Giang

Phu Tho   HANOI

Dien Bien Phu

Ha Tay   Hung
Yen
Ha Nam   Hai Phong

LAOS

Gulf
of
Tonkin

THAILAND

Hue

*Ha Tay province was merged with Hanoi in 2008

Traditional "category IV" tile roof village house.

Newer style cement roof village house.

Returning home for ceremonial obligations.

Returning home for agricultural work.

Long Bien wholesale market in the early-morning hours.

Leaving Long Bien wholesale market.

Cooking prepared foods along the bank of the Red River.

Setting off to start selling after cleaning and arranging fruit...

...and sometimes selling well into the evening.

Street vendors have to walk many miles each day...

...but they try to find safe places to stop and sell or just rest.

Early-morning street market, before police come to chase everyone away.

Later in the day, next to a "No Selling Allowed" sign.

Returning to her rooming house at the end of the day.

Long Bien rooming house area.

Back in her room, counting her money for the day.

Two street vendors get back to their room early and take time to chat...

...before preparing dinner out on the balcony for the rest of their group.

Appendix: The Literature About Migration

In this section we introduce some of the literature about migration, both the theoretical explanations of why people migrate and some of the empirical literature about migration in Vietnam. We compare what we know about roving street vendors with what the theories say about migration in general, and we also compare the migration of street vendors with the results of work on other types of migrants.

The theoretical model still most commonly used to explain internal migration began in 1970 with Harris and Todaro.[95] They argued, and the orthodox economic theory of internal migration continues to argue, that migration depends on differences between the rural and urban incomes that migrants can expect to earn. Expected income depends on a combination of two factors: the urban income multiplied by the probability of earning that income. That is, if rural people expect that they can earn more in the city than they could in the country, they will migrate to do so. In all of the theoretical economic models, income differentials–between rural and urban incomes–are the principal factor in the decision to migrate.

One difficulty with the Harris and Todaro model is that it originally did not include an informal sector, which led to the assumption that migrants who were unsuccessful in their search for work in the urban formal sector would become unemployed. Subsequent versions of the model did incorporate an urban informal sector, but they retained the assumption that migrants used it only as a stepping-stone to permanent employment in the urban formal sector.[96]

More recently, Ranis and Stewart updated the Harris and Todaro model by dividing the urban informal sector into a traditional informal sector and a modernizing informal sector.[97] The modernizing informal sector contributes to economic development by producing a broader variety of goods, including simple capital goods, thus making it possible for employees in the sector to enjoy rising incomes over time. According to Ranis and Stewart, the traditional informal sector acts like a "sponge," absorbing migrants to cities who cannot find employment in either the formal or the modernizing informal sectors. The traditional informal sector produces goods that are sold largely to low-income urban residents, and because it has no linkages to either the formal sector or the modernizing informal sector, Ranis and Stewart see the traditional informal sector as not contributing to the process of development.

In spite of the widespread acceptance of the Harris and Todaro model and its various incarnations in the realm of economic theory, we and others have expressed significant dissatisfaction with this model in terms of its ability to explain the many types of migration that take place in countries like Vietnam. First, the theory has a hard time explaining the gendered nature of many types of migration and why in some cases men are the ones to migrate whereas in other cases women migrate. Attempts to incorporate a prospective marriage partners variable into the model, in our view, fail to capture the gendered aspects of internal migration in all of their complexity.[98] This is all the more so in the case of migrant street vendors, most of whom are women who are already married.

Second, the Harris and Todaro model implicitly assumes that all internal migration is permanent (or at the very least long-term), and it is unable to explain why many forms of migration are of a more temporary nature. Circular migration is an example of this. In this book, we show that women who come to Hanoi as circular migrants do so precisely so that they and their families can maintain their rural identities. Therefore, we believe that circular migration should be recognized as an important alternative to permanent migration.

Finally, in spite of the more recent efforts of Ranis and Stewart to look at the urban informal sector in a different light, the neoclassical model fails to understand the full importance of this sector to the process of development in countries like Vietnam. First, our own work and that of others have shown that it is problematic to think of this sector in such strictly dichotomous terms as a modernizing informal sector and a traditional informal sector.[99] As is the case with many informal sector workers in countries around the world, street vendors in Vietnam sell their goods to customers in both the modern sector and in what Ranis and Stewart would call the traditional sector. Equally important, and as we show in this book, the income that most street vendors earn is tremendously important in improving the material conditions of their family lives. Because, as noted above, this income helps them maintain their rural identities, we argue that the informal sector plays a critical role in the fight against rural poverty. If they did not have these jobs, it is entirely possible that they and their families might be forced off the farm and into the cities. In this sense, forms of circular migration to work in the urban informal sector could be thought of as important in the fight against urban poverty as well.

Others have also recognized these problems with the economic theories of migration and have contributed different explanations for migration. Chant and Radcliffe[100] point out, similarly to the previous discussion, that the "neoclassical" theory—the Harris and Todaro framework—does not help explain why women are the most common street vendors or why in those families it is the woman, not the man who migrates. Nor does the neoclassical theory incorporate the various social and cultural structures that influence the migration decision. Of the four theories that Chant and Radcliffe discuss in their work, the household strategies approach seems to us the most useful.

The household strategies approach recognizes that migration occurs because of economic necessity, but it also takes into account the gender division of labor within the household. As Chant and Radcliffe argue, "… it is not enough simply to recognize that gender divisions of labour exist and can explain patterns of labour allocation within and beyond the household unit: the ways in which women (and men) are moulded by intra-household hierarchies of power and by wider socio-cultural expectations of gender also need consideration. Thus female migration experiences are determined both by intra-household resource and decision-making structures, and by the socially determined, gender-segregated labour markets available to them."[101]

While it is an improvement on the economic theories of migration, the household strategies approach has its own shortcomings when applied to roving street vendors. The gender roles constraints that Chant and Radcliffe discuss do not seem to affect the decision that street vendor families make, perhaps because street vendors are circular rather than permanent migrants. As we discuss, it is common for street vendors to take up traditional gender roles when they return to their villages, and it is also common for many husbands to have help from their children and their parents with household tasks and farming. Thus, we agree with Chant and Radcliffe that it is essential to account for many more issues than simply the need for more income. However, we show that in the case of street vendor families traditional gender roles do not constrain women's ability to migrate. We also show that the decision to migrate is very strongly influenced by socio-cultural norms and the results of family decision-making that incorporates a variety of factors particular to the family.

In terms of the empirical literature about migration in Vietnam, relatively little has been written on circular migration in general and female circular migration in particular even though this type of migration has become much more important since *Doi Moi*. Much of what has been written on this pattern of migration calls it temporary migration, a term that is too vague, we believe, to be analytically useful.[102] As Nguyen and White note, the principle reason for the lack of more studies on temporary migration is "the lack of data that is both adequate and accurate."[103] Some studies on internal migration are based on data taken from the census surveys or targeted surveys in a small number of places.[104] Unfortunately, there are no questions that ask specifically about circular migration in the censuses or in the bi-annual Vietnam Household Living Standards Surveys (VHLSS).[105] The 2004 Vietnam Migration Survey records only one of a person's possible many moves per year, thus reducing its usefulness for discussing seasonal or circular migration.[106] As a result, most of the literature on circular migration that does exist has been based largely on case studies, many of these looking at only one or two villages. Only a few look at female migrants from a greater number of villages within a larger region of the country. Some of these look at many different kinds of migrants,[107] while at least one focuses on women who work at one type of job.[108] The studies that look at female circular migrants who come from the same village tend to focus on women who all perform the same job. These include, most notably, studies of roving recyclers in Hanoi.[109]

Within the empirical literature, a number of interesting and important themes emerge. One is the importance of the need for income that is behind the decision to migrate. Another is the issue of permanence: whether those who migrate to the city intend to or ultimately do remain permanently. The importance of village norms and social networks in shaping patterns of migration is an issue that comes up in many of the case studies. There is also the issue of whether or not circular migrants come to the city only during periods of slack agricultural demand. Gender issues that result from these patterns of migration are a topic that is beginning to receive some (but in our view still not enough) attention. Finally, of great concern for the future of this and other informal sector sidewalk activities are the threats posed by efforts to modernize the city and by rising urban incomes.

Virtually all studies of temporary migration in Vietnam cite some type of economic reason that relates to the need for income as an important motivation for migration. This reason is expressed in terms such as "better economic prospects"[110] and "underemployment" and "low income" (referring to the rural situation).[111] As we showed in Chapter 2, economic reasons for migration also include the pressures imposed by increasingly expensive ceremonial obligations, mounting debt, and rising agricultural and educational expenses. Perhaps the strongest assertion of the importance attached to the need for extra income comes from de Brauw and Harigaya who attribute 91 percent of the growth in rural per capita average expenditure between 1993 and 1998 to seasonal migration. They "also find that without seasonal migration, the estimated poverty rate would have been three percentage points higher than it was in 1998."[112] Pham and Hill, along with Vu find, as we do, that income helps not only with survival of rural families but also with their ability to accumulate wealth.[113] With the exception of this book, however, most of the literature does not have any systematic or detailed analysis of the income earned from circular migration nor its importance to the families of migrants.

On the question of permanence, Li found that most of the migrants included in her study did not intend to stay in Hanoi permanently: 50 percent wanted to get a temporary job, while another 30 percent wanted a long-term (but not permanent) job. Only 19 percent said that they came to Hanoi in order to find a permanent job; the remaining one percent said that they came to Hanoi in the hope of getting married there. In most case studies, however, the issue of permanence does not even arise.[114] This is the result of their focus on circular migration, the very nature of which permits, as we discussed in detail in Chapter 2, families to have a foot in both places. Successful circular migration is a strategy that obviates the need for permanent relocation of any family members, so it is understandable that none of these studies mentions the issue of permanent migration.

Another theme that arises in the literature is how circular migrants allocate their time between working in the city and working at home. This theme is important in part because of the widely held popular belief among Hanoi residents that street vending is a job that is only done in periods of slack agricultural work and that because of this it is superfluous. Although Nguyen (2005) found that circular migrants did work their schedules around the agricultural calendar, and although it is true that circular migrants do return home to help out with agricultural tasks, other case studies recognize that there are many reasons why women return to their villages.[115] As we discussed in Chapter 2, among those reasons are the need to be present for a variety of ceremonies, especially weddings, funerals, and death anniversary celebrations; to care for their children or husband when they are ill; and simply to rest and be at home with their families whenever they are too tired from working in Hanoi. We have found that women often find it difficult to balance the competing pressures they are under: on the one hand to earn badly needed income for their families, and on the other to represent the family at important events in the village. The fact that, in 2007, we found that 17 percent of women had taken to hiring wage labor to do at least some agricultural work for them so that they could spend more time working in Hanoi shows the depth of the pressure to be away from the village. The complexity of reasons surrounding the back and forth movement of many circular migrants is an important reason why the term "seasonal" needs to be used very carefully.

Similar to what we discussed in Chapter 2, many of the other case studies highlight the important role that village norms and social networks play in shaping the terms under which most migrant women are able to work and live in the city. For example, the fact that it is highly unusual for a woman to leave her village and begin work in Hanoi entirely on her own is a response to what villagers believe is appropriate. Similarly, roving street vendors often go with or join in Hanoi other women from their village or commune, and these women typically live with each other in Hanoi.[116] These groups are an important resource for street vendors while in Hanoi. They provide psychological support for women who miss their families while living in crowded and difficult circumstances. Further, when the police confiscate one street vendor's goods and equipment, her group often provides loans to help the woman regain her ability to continue to sell.

Another aspect of village norms that some women cite for having to migrate is the pressure they feel to keep up with their neighbors.[117] Keeping up, as we discussed in Chapter 2, includes giving appropriately sized monetary gifts on ceremonial occasion, hosting comparable ceremonial meals, sending their children to extra classes, and having a house that does not stand out from others in the village. This pressure, in turn, adds to the economic reasons they have for migrating.

While gender issues in Vietnam have been extensively studied,[118] not enough has been written about gender in the context of migration. Vu is an important exception, and her work was explicitly designed to examine gender and migration over the course of women's lives in two Red River delta villages.[119] In their study of recylers from two communes in Nam Dinh province, Resurreccion and Ha do emphasize the increased burdens on women that result from circular migration.[120] They also look at how circular migration affects the nature of gender roles within the household. Nguyen Binh looks at this issue as well, but only in a single village in Hung Yen province.[121] In both of those studies, the authors found that when the women are working in Hanoi, husbands, parents-in-law, children, and others take over the tasks usually done by women when they are in the village. However, they also found this change of gender roles is only a temporary phenomenon: when the female circular migrants return home, they re-assume their expected and traditional duties.

141

References

Beresford, Melanie, "Vietnam: The Transition from Central Planning," in Garry Rodan, Kevin Hewison and Richard Robison, ed., *The Political Economy of South-East Asia*, Melbourne: Oxford University Press, 1997, 179-204.

Chant, S. and S. A. Radcliffe, "Migration and Development: The Importance of Gender," in S. Chant, ed., *Gender and Migration in Developing Countries*, London: Belhaven Press, 1992, 1-29.

Cling, Jean-Pierre, Le Van Duy, Nguyen Thi Thu Huyen, Phan T. Ngoc Tran, Mirielle Razafindrakoto, and Francois Roubaud, *Shedding light on a huge black hole: the informal sector in Hanoi*, GSO-ISS/IRD-DIAL project, April, 2009.

Cohen, Margot, "Neat Streets," *Far Eastern Economic Review*, *166*(21), 2003, 38.

Dang, Nguyen Anh and Duong Bach Le, "Women's Migration and Urban Integration in the Context of Doi Moi Economic Renovations," in Nguyen Anh Dang, ed., *Migration in Vietnam: Theoretical Approaches and Evidence from a Survey*, Hanoi: Transport Communication Publishing House, 2001, 73-91.

de Brauw, Alan and Tomoko Harigaya, "Seasonal Migration and Improving Living Standards in Vietnam," *American Journal of Agricultural Economics*, *89*(2), 2007, 430-447.

DiGregorio, Michael, *Urban Harvest: Recycling as a Peasant Industry in Northern Vietnam*, East-West Center Occasional Papers, Environment Series 17, Honolulu, Hawaii: East-West Center, 1994.

DiGregorio, Michael, Trinh Thi Tien, Nguyen Thi Hoang Lan, and Nguyen Thu Ha, "Linking Community and Small Enterprise Activities with Urban Waste Management: Hanoi Case Study," unpublished report, 1997.

Djamba, Yanyi, Alice Goldstein and Sidney Goldstein, "Permanent and Temporary Migration in Viet Nam During a Period of Economic Change," *Asia-Pacific Population Journal*, *14*(3), 1999, 25-48.

Drummond, Lisa, "Street Scenes: Practices of Public and Private Space in Urban Vietnam," *Urban Studies*, 37, 12: 2377-2391, 2000.

Fforde, Adam and Stefan de Vylder, *From Plan to Market: The Economic Transition in Vietnam*, Westview Press, 1996.

General Statistical Office, *Census Monograph on Internal Migration and Urbanization in Viet Nam*, Hanoi: Statistical Publishing House, 2001.

General Statistical Office, *Results of the Survey on Households Living Standards 2002*, Hanoi: Statistical Publishing House, 2004.

General Statistical Office, *Viet Nam Living Standards Survey, 1997-1998*, Hanoi: Statistical Publishing House, 2000.

General Statistical Office, *Vietnam Household Living Standards Survey*, various years.

General Statistics Office (GSO) and United Nations Population Fund, *The 2004 Vietnam Migration Survey: Internal Migration and Related Life Course Events*, Hanoi: UNFPA, 2006.

Ha, Tien Phuong Thi and Ha Quang Ngoc, *Female Labor Migration, Rural-Urban*, Hanoi: Women's Publishing House, 2001.

Harris, John R. and Michael P. Todaro, "Migration, Unemployment, and Development: A Two-Sector Analysis," *American Economic Review*, 60, 1970, 126-142.

Hoang Xuan Thanh, Dang Nguyen Anh, and Cecilia Tacoli, *Livelihood Diversification and Rural-Urban Linkages in Vietnam's Red River Delta*, FCND Discussion Paper 193, Washington, DC: International Food Policy Research Institute, 2005.

Hoang, Thinh Ba, *Vai Tro Cua Nguoi Phu Nu Nong Thon Trong Cong Nghiep Hoa Nong Nghiep (Nghien Cuu Khu Vuc Dong Bang Song Hong)*, Hanoi: Nha Xuat Ban Chinh Tri Quoc Gia, 2002.

Huard, Pierre et Maurice Durand, <u>Connaissance du Viet-nam</u>, Paris: Imprimerie Nationale pour Ecole Francaise d'Extreme-Orient, 1954.

Jensen, Rolf, *Street Vendors: three films by Rolf Jensen.* Hanoi: Vietnamese Women's Museum, 2012.

Jensen, Rolf and Donald M. Peppard Jr., "A Case Study of Roving Street Vendors," *Journal of Asian and African Studies, 38*(1), 2003, 71-84.

Jensen, Rolf and Donald M. Peppard Jr., "Food-Buying Habits in Hanoi," *Sojourn, 22*(2), 2007, 230-254.

Jensen, Rolf and Donald M. Peppard Jr., "The Traditional Brickmaking Industry and the Rural Economy of Vietnam," *Journal of Asian and African Studies, 39*(3), 2004, 193-207.

Kerkvliet, Benedict J. Tria, "Surveying Local Government and Authority in Contemporary Vietnam," in Benedict J. Tria and David G. Marr Kerkvliet, ed., *Beyond Hanoi: Local Government in Vietnam,* Singapore: Institute of Southeast Asian Studies, 2004, 1-27.

Knodel, John, Vu Manh Loi, Rukmalie Jayakody, and Vu Tuan Huy, *Gender Roles in the Family: Change and Stability in Vietnam,* Population Studies Center at the Institute for Social Research, University of Michigan, Report No. 04-559, Ann Arbor, MI: Population Studies Center at the Institute for Social Research, University of Michigan, 2004.

Koh, David Wee Hock, *Wards of Hanoi,* Singapore: Institute of Southeast Asian Studies, 2006.

Lautier, Bruno, *L'economie Informelle dans le Tiers Monde,* Paris: Editions La Decouvverte, 1994.

Lavoie, Mylene, *Women and Microcredit in Vietnam, Field Report 1999-2000,* Anthropology Department, Laval University, 2002.

Li, Tana, *Peasants on the Move: Rural-Urban Migration in the Hanoi Region,* Singapore: Institute for Southeast Asian Studies, 1996.

Luong, Hy V., "Gender Relations: Ideologies, Kinship Practices, and Political Economy," in Hy V. Luong, ed., *Postwar Vietnam: Dynamics of a Transforming Society,* Lanham, Maryland: Rowman and Littlefield, 2003, 201-223.

Marsh, S. P., T.G. MacAulay, and P. V. Hung, "Taxes and Land Use, in Sally P. Marsh, T.Gordon MacAulay, and Pham Van Hung, eds., *Agricultural Development and Land Policy in Vietnam: Policy Briefs.*, ACIAR Monograph No. 126, Canberra: Australian Centre for International Agricultural Research, 2007.

Nguyen, Binh Thanh Thi, ""Di Cho" or Going to Market: A Pattern of Seasonal Migration and Transition in a Northern Vietnamese Village," diss, International School for Humanities and Social Sciences: Universiteit van Amsterdam, 2001.

Nguyen, Cham Phuong Thi, "The Voices of Trinh Xa Women Who Earn Money for a Living in Hanoi," New Voices from the Mekong Region: Women in the Public Arena, Chiang Mai University, Chiang Mai Thailand, November 7-10, 2005, 2005.

Nguyen, Liem T., and Michael J. White, "Health Status of Temporary Migrants in Urban Areas in Vietnam," *International Migration*, 45(4), 2007, 101-133.

Nguyen, Liem Thanh, "Intentions of Temporary Migrants to Stay in Urban Areas," in Anh Nguyen Dang, ed., *Migration in Vietnam: Theoretical Approaches and Evidence from a Survey*, Hanoi: Transport Communication Publishing House, 2001, 145-177.

Painter, Martin, "The Politics of State Sector Reforms in Vietnam: Contested Agendas and Uncertain Trajectories," *Journal of Development Studies*, 41(2), 2005, 261-283.

Pettus, Ashley, *Between Sacrifice and Desire: National Identity and the Governing of Femininity in Vietnam*, New York: Routledge, 2003.

Pham, Nguyen Bang, and Peter S. Hill, "The Role of Temporary Migration in Rural Household Economic Strategy in a Transitional Period for the Economy of Vietnam," *Asian Population Studies,* 4(1), 2008, 57-75.

Poverty Task Force, *Red River Delta Ha Tay and Hai Duong, Participatory Poverty Assessment*, Hanoi: World Bank, 2003.

Poverty Task Force, *Regional Poverty Assessment, Red River Delta Region,* 2005, Hanoi: World Bank, 2005.

Ranis, Gustav, and Frances Stewart, "V-Goods and the Role of the Urban Informal Sector in Development," *Economic Development and Cultural Change, 47,* 1999, 259-288.

Resurreccion, Bernadette P., and Ha Thi Van Khanh, "Able to Come and Go: Reproducing Gender in Female Rural-Urban Migration in the Red River Delta," *Population, Space and Place, 13*(3), 2007, 211-224.

Scott, Stephanie, Truong Thi Kim Chuyen, "Behind the Numbers: Social Mobility, Regional Disparities, and New Trajectories of Development in Rural Vietnam," in Philip Taylor, ed., *Social Inequality in Vietnam and the Challenges to Reform,* Singapore: Institute of Southeast Asia Studies, 2004, 90-122.

Shuler, Sidney Ruth et al., "Construction of Gender in Vietnam: In Pursuit of the 'Three Criteria'," *Culture, Heath, and Sexuality, 8*(5), 2006, 383-394.

Thadani, Veena N., and Michael P. Todaro, *Female Migration in Developing Countries: A Framework for Analysis,* New York: Population Council, 1979.

Todaro, Michael P., "Internal Migration in Developing Countries: A Survey," in Michael P. Todaro, ed., *Reflections on Economic Development,* Hants, England: Edward Elgar, 1995.

Tran, Ha Thu, Tran Tuan, Trudy Harpham, Pham Thi Lan, Tran Duc Thach, Sharon Huttly, and Anne McCoy, *Extra Classes and Learning Outcomes of Eight-Year-Old Children in Vietnam,* London: Young Lives, 2005.

Turner, Sarah, and Laura Schoenberger, "Street Vendor Livelihoods and Everyday Politics in Hanoi, Vietnam: The Seeds of a Diverse Economy?" *Urban Studies,* 49 (5), April, 2012, 1027-1044.

UNDP, *Expanding Choices for the Rural Poor,* Hanoi: UNDP, 1998.

United Nations Viet Nam, *Internal Migration and Socio-economic Development in Viet Nam: A Call to Action,* HaNoi, July, 2010.

Van Arkadie, Brian and Raymond Mallon, *Viet Nam—a Transition Tiger?* Australian National University: Asia Pacific Press, 2003.

Vietnam News, "Ha Noi to clear its footpaths of traders," July 15, 2003, p. 3.

Vu, Thao Thi, "Making a Living in Rural Vietnam from (Im)mobile Livelihoods: a Case of Women's Migration," *Population, Space and Place,* (online) 2012.

Werner, Jayne, "Gender, Household, and State: Renovation (Doi Moi) as Social Process in Viet Nam," in Jayne Werner, and Daniele Belanger, ed., *Gender, Household, State: Doi Moi in Viet Nam*, Ithaca, New York: Southeast Asia Program, Cornell University, 2002, 29-47.

Werner, Jayne, *Gender, Household, and State in Post-Revolutionary Vietnam*, New York: Routledge, 2009.

Wisensale, Steven T., "Marriage and Family Law in a Changing Vietnam," *Journal of Family Issues,* 20, 1999, 602-616.

World Bank, *Vietnam Country Gender Assessment*, in *Vietnam Country Gender Assessment*, World Bank, 2006.

World Bank, *Vietnam Development Report 2004: Poverty*, World Bank, 2003.

Web sites

Ecolex:http://www.ecolex.org/ecolex/ledge/view/RecordDetails;document_R esolution%20No.%2055/2010/QH12%20on%20agricultural%2 0land%20use%20tax%20exemption%20and%20reduction..html? DIDPFDSIjsessionid=784361CBF5932206B86E86DC59154E9 8?id=LEX-FAOC100803&index=documents accessed 28 Feb 2012 Text of Resolution 55/2010/QH12

General Statistical Office,
Http://www.gso.gov.vn/default_en.aspx?tabid=472&idmid=3&Ite mID=5175.

http://www.gso.gov.vn/default_en.aspx?tabid=515&idmid=5&Ite mID=9813 (2009 Census) accessed 13 June 2012

http://www.vietbiz24.com/Articles/1023/18729/legal/vietnam-congress-passes-agricultural-land-use-tax-exemptions.aspx accessed 8 June 2012

Vietnam News, "City Officials Open Markets to Bidding," Vietnam News, 25/9 2004, http://vietnamnews.vnagency.com.vn/2004-09/24/Stories/06.htm.

Vietnam News, "Domestic Retailers Urged to Think Big," Vietnam News, 10/03 2006, <http://vietnamnews.vnagency.com.vn/showarticle.php?num=03B US100306>.

Vietnam News, "Ha Noi Municipal Authorities Call for a Cleaner, Greener Capital City," Vietnam News, 02/05 2006, <http://vietnamnews.vnagency.com.vn/showarticle.php?num=05S OC020506>.

Vietnam News, "Ha Noi to Take up Charge of Markets," Vietnam News, 28/10 2005, <http://vietnamnews.vnagency.com.vn/showarticle.php?num=01B US281005>.

World Bank, http://data.worldbank.org/indicator, accessed 9 February 2012

World Bank, http://data.worldbank.org/indicator/SE.ENR.TERT.FM.ZS

World Bank, http://data.worldbank.org/indicator, accessed 9 February 2012

World Bank,
http://data.worldbank.org/indicator/SE.ENR.SECO.FM.ZS/coun
tries/VN-4E-XN?display=graph, accessed 8 June 2012

World Bank,
http://databank.worldbank.org/Data/Views/Reports/TableView.as
px?IsShared=true&IsPopular=country accessed, 11 June 2012

World Bank,
http://databank.worldbank.org/ddp/home.do?Step=2&id=4&hAc
tiveDimensionId=WDI_Series, accessed 1 June 2012

World Bank,
http://databank.worldbank.org/Data/Views/Reports/TableView.as
px?IsShared=true&IsPopular=country, accessed 11 June 2012

Notes

[1] Hanoi is located in the Red River Delta region of Vietnam. Comprised of 11 provinces in the northeastern part of Vietnam, in 2009, the delta had almost 23 percent of the population of Vietnam but only 6 percent of the land area, (General Statistical Office, 2009, http://www.gso.gov.vn/default_en.aspx?tabid=515&idmid=5&ItemID=9813 (accessed 13 June 2012) making it the most densely populated of the six socioeconomic regions in Vietnam. The Red River Delta also has the second lowest total land area for agriculture, but its two major cities–Hanoi and Hai Phong--employ about 80 percent of formal sector employees in the delta. The percentage of the total population in the delta that is urban is about the same as for the country as a whole. (Poverty Task Force, 2005: 1-2)

[2] Cong Thong Tin Dien Tu, gis.chinhphu.vn, accessed 10 March 2013

[3] Of course, we are not the only ones to make note of this: "People are coming to use public spaces for more personal expression...; and encroachment for personal or commercial use (pavement stalls, the spilling out of wares from cramped shops and 'pay parking' for motorcycles and bicycles)." (Drummond, 2000:2382)

[4] There are many definitions of "informal," but all mention that this is a sector of the economy to which many government rules and regulations do not apply. Definitions usually also include its ease of entry and that it is often made up of very small (fewer than 10 employees) firms or self-employed individuals. Cling et al., define the informal sector as "...all unregistered unincorporated enterprises (called informal household businesses)..." and go on to say that the results of a government survey in 2007 estimate that the informal sector in Hanoi provided 30% of all jobs. (Cling et al., 2009: 3) Painter estimates that the informal sector in Vietnam may comprise about 50 percent of the total economy. (Painter, 2005: 268)

[5] Many people call them "basket ladies" because they are women and because the baskets hanging from their poles are their most easily identifiable feature. Throughout the book, we use "roving street vendors" and "basket ladies" interchangeably.

[6] UNDP, 1998

[7] In 2000, we found that 44 percent of roving vendors were circular migrants, 38 percent were daily migrants, and the remainder were Hanoi residents. (Jensen and Peppard, 2003:73)

[8] Because of the wealth of other sources about Vietnam's economic problems and later reforms, in this section we attempt to give only a very brief overview. For more on Vietnam's reform program, see Beresford, 1997, for a short summary, or Fforde and DeVylder, 1996, and Van Arkadie and Mallon, 2003, for more detailed discussions.

[9] See Beresford, 1997, and Van Arkadie and Mallon, 2003.

[10] Van Arkadie and Mallon, 2003.

[11] Van Arkadie and Mallon, 2003:34

[12] World Bank, 2003. http://databank.worldbank.org/Data/Views/Reports/TableView.aspx?IsShared=true&IsPopular=country (accessed 11 June 2012)

[13] World Bank, http://databank.worldbank.org/ddp/home.do?Step=2&id=4&hActiveDimensionId=WDI_Series (accessed 11 June 2012)

[14] Ibid.

[15] See Kerkvliet, 2004, and Van Arkadie and Mallon, 2003.

[16] Koh, 2006: 156, 192 (note 2)

[17] Werner, 2002

[18] Vietnam News, July 15, 2003:3

[19] Koh, 2006: chapter 4

[20] Jensen and Peppard, 2007

[21] In spite of some serious remaining problems, Vietnam has been successful in efforts to promote some aspects of gender equality: "Vietnam was one of the first countries to sign and ratify the Convention on the Elimination

of all forms of Discrimination Against Women (CEDAW) in 1980 and 1982. Prior to CEDAW, Vietnam embodied the principle of equality of men and women in the Constitution of Vietnam. The 1992 amendments to the constitution paid close attention to gender equality considerations. The newly issued Gender Equality Law provides leverage for addressing priority gender issues." (World Bank, 2006: 25) "With one of the highest rates of economic participation of women in the world, and the highest participation of women in parliament in the Asia Pacific Region, Vietnam is one of the more advanced countries with respect to gender equality. The country has appropriate policies to ensure equal rights of men and women and very significant progress has been made in reducing the gender gaps in health and education, and improving the situation of women more generally."(World Bank, 2006: 5)

[22] Huard et Durand, 1954: 94-95

[23] There may also have been a slight gender bias, but it is hard to discern this from the interviews that we conducted. Virtually all rural families were poor, the street vendors say, and most children, boys and girls alike, quit school after middle school and did not go on to high school. Today, upper secondary (high school) enrollment rates are equal for boys and girls. (World Bank, http://databank.worldbank.org/Data/Views/Reports/TableView.aspx?IsShared=true&IsPopular=country (accessed 11 June 2012))

[24] Arranged marriages were among the customs that were made illegal in the North under the Marriage and Family Law of 1959. (Wisensale, 1999: 604)

[25] The Vietnamese lunar year is not a pure one and is made to correspond to the solar year by inserting an additional month every two or three years. This intercalary, or leap, month is given the same number as the preceding month. The lunar leap years occur in such a way as to guarantee that the winter solstice will always fall sometime in the 11th lunar month, meaning that Tet will always be in January or February. In this book, we refer, as street vendors themselves do, to lunar months, but an approximate correlation to the solar calendar is to add 1 to the number of any particular lunar month. For example, the 8th lunar month usually corresponds approximately to the month of September.

[26] In 2001, only about 13 percent of street vendors did not work in Hanoi during the first lunar month; in 2003, 23 percent took that month off

from work in Hanoi; and in 2006, we found that only 16 percent had been home for the entire first month.

[27] See Huard et Durand, 1954:78-81 for a description of these and other lunar holidays.

[28] The practice of giving cash gifts at ceremonial meals is a relatively recent one that has replaced the more traditional practice of giving gifts in kind. Typically, people gave gifts of a kilogram of sugar, a can of condensed milk, fruit, and other goods when they attended a ceremony. Most women say that the change to cash gifts took place sometime after the implementation of Doi Moi. While they are not sure of the reasons for the change, they speak of the advantages that cash gifts have over gifts that usually perished before a family could finish consuming them.

[29] Further on, we discuss how the gifts associated with each ceremony form part of a set of mutual gift obligations on the part of rural families. Because gifts received must be reciprocated at some point in the future, the increase in village giving norms has the effect of preserving at least some of the real value of cash gifts over time. The phenomenon of rising costs of hosting "life-cycle" ceremonies has been noted by Luong, who attributes more elaborate ceremonies to "the need of households to maintain their informal networks of reciprocity, which could be mobilized in times of need." (Luong, 2003:212)

[30] For those families that incurred the expenses in the year prior to the VHLSS survey, both wedding and funeral expenses were much higher in 2008 than they were in 2002: median wedding costs had jumped about 40 times, but median funeral costs had risen only 2.5 times. (Authors' calculations from VHLSS 2002 and 2008.)

[31] Often this is for menial jobs that do not require any technical skills. Doing things like operating a power tool such as a drill often requires a degree from a technical training school in addition to the high school diploma.

[32] In some villages, retired teachers may offer supplemental classes of their own. In these cases, the coercive nature of the fees is considerably lessened, so parents who pay them do so because they have confidence in the teacher and because they believe the courses will benefit their children. Still, the majority of extra classes are offered by a child's own

teacher, a practice that is widespread throughout the country. While it has become something of a national outrage for some, to date little has been done about it. "Teachers are the main suppliers of extra classes, which often take place in their houses after official school hours. Teachers use different ways of pressuring students to take extra classes, such as assigning difficult exercises, teaching official lessons very fast, and discriminating against those students who do not take extra lessons. Extra classes can therefore become a mechanism through which civil servants us their position for private gain... Unauthorized extra classes have been officially banned by the government. Various legal documents have been promulgated to halt the situation, such as Decree No.242/TTg concerning regulations for extra classes which was approved by the Prime Minister in 1993, and a number of circulars. However, they appear to have had no impact." (Tran et al., 2005:5)

[33] The principal exception involves the eldest son of the family. He and his wife are often expected to live with the parents even after they form an independent household. They will then take care of the parents as they get older and will inherit the house when the parents die.

[34] Ha and Ha also note that one of the pressures that drives rural people to migrate to cities for work is to enable them to catch up to their neighbors. (Ha and Ha, 2001: 170)

[35] In the rural provinces of the Red River Delta, the cost per square meter of building a house in the year prior to the survey about doubled between 2002 and 2008. (Authors' calculations from VHLSS 2002 and 2008.)

[36] It also means that this person is likely to refuse to accept the money if the one who has borrowed it tries to pay it back before it is asked for.

[37] As this book goes to press in early 2013, Vietnam's land law is under revision, with a final version expected in mid-year. The government has announced that existing land use rights will automatically extend until the law is final, and the press is suggesting that the term of use rights may extend to 50 years. We have seen no discussion of a new allocation of land. (Asia Sentinel, http://www.asiasentinel.com/index.php?option=com_content&task=view&id=5165&Itemid=213 (accessed 14 March 2013; Trust Law, http://www.trust.org/trustlaw/news/vietnam-land-law-revision-should-improve-fairness-transparency-analysts/ (accessed 14 March 2013)

[38] In a few cases, children were allocated less land than adult family members, and in one commune that we know of only adult family members received land.

[39] A sao is the basic unit of land measurement that varies across the northern, central, and southern regions of Vietnam. Throughout the northern region of the country where the street vendors of this study all reside, it is equal to 360 square meters. This is slightly less than 1/10th of an acre; in terms of hectares, there are just under 28 sao per hectare.

[40] This conclusion is somewhat at odds with the results of the 2002 VHLSS, which found that the poorest quintile of households had an average annual crop land holding of 4778 square meters, which is more than 13 sao; the next poorest quintile had about 11 sao per household (World Bank, 2003: 40). We are concerned about this discrepancy but stand by the findings of our own surveys, interviews, and site visits.

[41] See, for example, the assertion that among the factors that trap people in poverty is "[l]ittle land resource because the land has been allocated for 20 years; new family members are not eligible for land; hence, household land cannot provide jobs and income for its members." (Poverty Task Force, 2003: 25)

[42] A concern for food security also helps explain circular migration of the type we discuss here because it helps families avoid the need to sell rice in order to have money for living expenses. (Hoang, Dang, and Tacoli, 2005:31)

[43] In Phu Tho and other provinces that lie just outside of the Red River Delta, the season starts somewhat earlier and most rice is transplanted either at the end of the 11th lunar month or later on in the 12th lunar month. This is because irrigated agriculture is less widespread outside of the delta, so rice needs to be planted earlier to take advantage of the winter rains. The typical rice crop takes about 100 days between planting and harvest.

[44] Data from the 2010 VHLSS show that in a long list of possible expenditures on rice and other crops, chemical fertilizer is by far the largest item. (Authors' calculation.)

[45] Marsh, MacAulay, and Hung, 2007: 15-16

[46] http://www.vietbiz24.com/Articles/1023/18729/legal/vietnam-congress-passes-agricultural-land-use-tax-exemptions.aspx (accessed 8 June 2012)

[47] In 2010, in the rural provinces of the Red River Delta, about 50 percent of surveyed households incurred expenses for "outsourced labor." (VHLSS 2010, authors' calculations.)

[48] While one of the reasons for the increased use of agricultural wage labor comes from the growing cash needs of the women who hire them, the other reason is the recent growth of an agricultural wage labor force itself. Street vendors themselves think that this is one of the results of the land shortage problem.

[49] This is significant in part because of the importance given to animal raising as part of the fight against rural poverty. For example, one of the groups identified as doing better than other groups included those who had diversified their agricultural income by "shifting to cash crops or animal production." (Poverty Task Force, 2003:21)

[50] Others have also noted the use of pig-raising as a means of saving, even though profits are low or non-existent. (Hoang, Dang, and Tacoli, 2005:17)

[51] This is understandable since chickens require relatively little attention, whereas the labor time required to bring ducks to water each day is much higher.

[52] In 2002, the survey asked two questions about debt, one of which, in the context of household expenditures, included mention of lending as well as debt payments in the past 12 months, thus making it of no use in trying to determine indebtedness; the second question asked only about borrowing in the previous 12 months. In 2004, the expenditure question did not include lending but still asked only about payments in the previous 12 months, and the second question again elicited information only about debt incurred in the previous 12 months. In 2010, there were still only two questions about debt, one of which asked, in the context of agricultural expenses, about interest paid in the past year, and the other asked only about borrowing from "preferential credit schemes."

[53] General Statistical Office, 2004:197

[54] Authors' calculation from VHLSS 2004 data.

[55] VHLSS 2010, authors' calculations

56 World Bank, 2003:42

57 The money for these loans comes from renting out 5 sao of commune-owned rice fields to private farmers at a rate of VND200,000 per sao per year. Similar programs have been reported in other communes throughout the region and are cited under the category of "socio-political organizations" in the VHLSS as a common source of lending to the poor. (General Statistical Office, 2004:197)

58 While most families are in possession of their "red book," a common problem for many had been that the LUC contained only the name of the husband and not the wife. This meant that in the event of the death or disappearance of a husband, the wife had no legal claim to the family land. The government has been conducting a public awareness campaign about this issue, and most street vendors now say that their names are listed along with their husbands'.

59 According to the Vietnam Development Report, the average rate charged by informal lenders is approximately 4 percent per month (World Bank 2003:43). Because most family relatives and many close friends do not charge any interest at all and because many other village lenders were reported to charge an interest rate equal to the prevailing bank rate, we found nothing close to this figure as an average interest rate from our own interviews. A rate of 4 percent per month is much closer to what a professional moneylender might charge, but most of the women we asked said that borrowing from these people is less prevalent in their villages now than it used to be.

60 For example, more than half of the families who borrowed money to invest did so to raise pigs, and we have already argued that the odds of just breaking even or even losing some money from this activity are high. Other reasons varied but included, for example, borrowing to help a son get into the army or to get a job, neither of which was likely to generate enough income to help the families pay back their debts.

61 We want to make clear that what street vendors tell us about debt burdens is understood as a more general problem among rural people: "...it [credit for urgent needs] can be a trap for borrowers. If they lack the extra money to pay urgent expenses, which is usually the case, where will they find the money to do the loan repayments? Often unable to repay their loans, when and if a new emergency occurs, they will have to take another loan, sinking even deeper into debt." (Lavoie, 2002: 14)

[62] While there is evidence throughout the country of people defaulting on their loans (World Bank 2003:43), we did not find this to be the case among the women included in our study.

[63] Jensen and Peppard, 2003

[64] The take-home income figures in Table 3.1 are equivalent to remittances that are discussed in the literature when looking at permanent migration. A street vendor's take-home income is the amount that she has left over at the end of the work-day. We begin with the profit that she earns on her sales, and then we subtract her costs of food and lodging while living in Hanoi.

[65] 1998 poverty levels from General Statistical Office, 2000: 260. We calculate the 2002 basic needs poverty level by adjusting the 1998 level for inflation. Because there was no inflation between 1998 and 1999, we are able to look at our own income data for 1999 in terms of these thresholds.

[66] The percentage of the rural population living at or below the food poverty threshold fell to 11.9 percent in 2002. The percentage of the rural population living at or below the General Poverty Line (a threshold that replaced the basic needs poverty line) that year was 35.6 percent. (GSO 2000:263; GSO 2004:25, 193) We argue, as do de Brauw and Harigaya, 2007, and Hoang, Dang, and Tacoli, 2005, that part of the reason behind this improvement in rural poverty rates is due to the incomes earned from informal sector activities like those performed by roving street vendors.

[67] Because of the way in which the data were collected, the 1998 distribution of income is measured in terms of per capita expenditure quintiles rather than income quintiles. For the purposes of our analysis here, this "measurement problem" is not significant. Since most women use the money they make to help meet family expenses, looking at this income in terms of expenditure quintiles instead of income quintiles is not a problem.

[68] Because we are measuring changes in income from each of the quintile means, the percent changes remain the same.

[69] General Statistical Office, http://www.gso.gov.vn/default_en.aspx?tabid=472&idmid=3&ItemID=5 175 (accessed 11 June 2012)

[70] We do not have systematic data on street vendor annual incomes after 2002, so these numbers are not completely comparable to the figures in Table 3.1. However, the upward trend for daily income is clear, and we are confident of our conclusion about real income.

[71] Jensen and Peppard, 2004

[72] The median age of the youngest child in these families was 6, and in only one of them were there no children 18 years or under living at home.

[73] These answers lend further support to the idea that a woman's domestic responsibilities increasingly include earning a cash income for the family. (Luong, 2003: 220) Resurreccion and Ha, 2007, heard similar responses in their case study.

[74] This is an important point in and of itself, but it is also important because of the widely held perception by people in Hanoi that roving street vendors come to the city when they do because they have nothing better to do back home. (Jensen and Peppard, 2007)

[75] The fact that a street vendor stops working in Hanoi at some point after she becomes pregnant does not necessarily mean that she stays home to rest. A 2002 study of the role of rural women in the Red River Delta found that more than 67 percent continued to work on their agricultural fields right up until they gave birth, and 80 percent continued to carry heavy loads. (Hoang, 2002: 176)

[76] This corresponds to the Vietnamese age of four years.

[77] In 2006, for example, five percent of those street vendors with children living at home said that their children generally took care of themselves while they were away. This was more than the three percent who said that their own parents (and not their husbands') took on this responsibility.

[78] Indeed, because Table 3.4 includes many families with only very young children (21 percent had children who were all less than seven years old), we suspect that the importance of children here may be underestimated.

[79] It is important to note that we do not simply assume that the duties to which we refer belong traditionally to women: the evidence is quite strong that the household duties that we discuss in this section are in fact most commonly done by women. See, for example, Knodel et al., 2004.

[80] This suggests that with the exception of chores related to supervising children, the only reason they do perform those tasks when their wives are gone is because there is nobody else at home to perform them instead.

[81] See Li, 1996, for example.

[82] Resurreccion and Ha, 2007; Nguyen, Binh, 2001.

[83] As far back as 1993, Li noted the noted the same kinds of things that we continued to hear about the importance of village social networks for circular migrants living and working in Hanoi: "They look after each other, carry letters and money to the folks at home, and lend and borrow money among themselves. Traditional, rural values have moved into the city with the migrants and are retained through the spontaneous clustering of their habitat." (Li, 1996: 45)

[84] Jensen & Peppard, 2007

[85] In 1997, bicycles were 30 percent of passenger traffic. (Koh, 2006: 161)

[86] Roving street vendors find themselves caught up in an administrative hierarchy of the municipal government of Hanoi whose rules and regulations aimed at getting roving street vendors off the streets and out of the city are often at odds with national government policy which recognizes that farm families cannot survive on agriculture alone and that the eradication of rural poverty requires that peasant farmers engage in non-farm income earning activities. DiGregorio, et al. discuss the contradictory effects of similar government attempts to restrict or eliminate the activity of roving recycling buyers, who are also mostly women and who perform the badly needed function of helping to reduce the amount of waste that enters Hanoi's landfills. (Cited in World Bank, 2003: 32) From our observations over the past 12 years, however, we see more stringent enforcement against street vendors who sell fruit and vegetables than against recyclers.

[87] See Cohen, 2003, for example.

[88] An interesting anecdote is that while roving street vendors virtually disappeared from the streets of Hanoi during the SEA Games, photographs of them were featured prominently in an official travel brochure that was prepared for foreign tourists attending the games. The

photographs were clearly intended to illustrate some of the "charm" that the city of Hanoi had to offer.

[89] The surveys we conducted in 2000 and in 2003 collected income data for 1999 and 2002, respectively. Data concerning living costs in Hanoi, however, were current for the years in which the surveys were conducted.

[90] Taylor (2007:14) echoes Li (1996) when he discusses the contradictory views of city dwellers toward spontaneous migrants from rural areas. While some urban people reported to Taylor that they were sympathetic to the plight of rural migrants, they also held strongly negative opinions. Taylor uses the same term that Li does—"ruralization"—to describe what city dwellers see happening to cities, and their depictions of this process use the same words-- "deterioration in the order, civility, and morality of their neighborhoods and public places"--that we discovered in our survey in 2004. This discussion in Taylor occurs in the context of permanent migration resulting from high rural unemployment and slow rural industrialization, which are some of the same reasons that temporary migrants come to Hanoi's informal sector for work.

[91] Jensen and Peppard, 2007

[92] Cling et al., (2009:14-15)

[93] The idea that the informal sector is here to stay has been made quite forcibly by the team that participated in the GSO/IRD-DIAL project on the informal sector in Vietnam. See, for example, Cling et al. 2010.

[94] Fforde and de Vylder, 1996

[95] Harris and Todaro, 1970

[96] Todaro, 1995: 109, 113

[97] Ranis and Stewart, 1999

[98] Thadani and Todaro, 1979

[99] See Jensen and Peppard, 2003, and also Lautier, 1994, and DiGregorio, 1994: 28-32.

161

[100] Chant and Radcliffe, 1992

[101] Ibid: 23

[102] Chant and Radcliffe, for example, discuss four types of temporary migration: seasonal, oscillating, relay, and circular/return. Further, they admit that different authors use the terms differently. Our use of circular corresponds to what Chant and Radcliffe call oscillating: this type of migration can take place at any time, and it involves repeated absences from home of relatively short periods. Chant and Radcliffe, 1992: 10-11

[103] Nguyen and White, 2007: 106. Referring to national census data and other national surveys, the United Nations Viet Nam notes that "[w]hile these large-scale surveys seek to be representative of the entire population, it is important to acknowledge that some types of migration, including movements by arguably the most vulnerable internal migrants in Viet Nam, are not being captured. This includes data on short-term, seasonal and return migration." (United Nations Viet Nam, 2010: 5)

[104] See Dang and Le, 2001, UNDP, 1998, and GSO 2006, for example.

[105] "... the census typically does not classify as migrants most temporary and seasonal movers." General Statistical Office, 2001: 6. The 2009 Census does not mention that issue, but its questions seem to be the same as those used in 1999.

[106] General Statistics Office, 2006. (Note that sometime in the previous decade, the GSO changed its name.)

[107] Li, 1996, Pham and Hill, 2008, and Vu, 2012

[108] Jensen and Peppard, 2003

[109] DiGregorio, 1994; Resurreccion and Ha, 2007; Nguyen, 2005

[110] Djamba, Goldstein, and Goldstein, 1999: Table 6

[111] Li, 1996: 33

[112] de Brauw and Harigaya, 2007: 444

[113] Pham and Hill, 2008, and Vu, 2012

[114] Li, 1996; Resurreccion and Ha, 2007; Nguyen, Thanh, 2001; Nguyen, 2005

[115] Nguyen, 2005: 2; Resurreccion and Ha, 2007

[116] Dang and Le, 2001: 80; DiGregorio, 1994; Li, 1996; Nguyen, 2001

[117] Ha and Ha, 2001: 170

[118] See Scott and Truong, 2007.

[119] Vu, 2012

[120] Resurreccion and Ha, 2007

[121] Nguyen, 2001

Photo Credits

cover photo
> courtesy of Nguyễn Hồng Hải

Street vendors have to walk many miles each day...
> courtesy of Nguyễn Hồng Hải

Later in the day, next to a "No Selling Allowed" sign.
> courtesy of Nguyễn Hồng Hải

Returning to her rooming house at the end of the day.
> courtesy of Vietnamese Women's Museum, Hanoi

Back in her room, counting her money for the day.
> courtesy of Phạm Xuân Thịnh

all other photos by Rolf Jensen

Map created by the authors using an outline map from d-Maps.com.

WOMEN ON THE MOVE

Chịu trách nhiệm xuất bản:
Giám đốc NGUYỄN THỊ TUYẾT

Chịu trách nhiệm bản thảo:
Phó Giám đốc - Tổng biên tập KHÚC THỊ HOA PHƯỢNG

Biên tập:	Lê Thu Ngọc
	Nguyễn Phương Quỳnh
Bìa:	Rolf Jensen
Trình bày:	Phạm Phượng
Sửa bản in:	Thu Ngọc

NHÀ XUẤT BẢN PHỤ NỮ

39 Hàng Chuối - Hà Nội.
ĐT: (04) 39717979 - 39717980 - 39710717 - 39716727 - 39712832.
FAX: (04) 39712830
E-mail: nxbphunu@vnn.vn
Website: www.nxbphunu.com.vn

Chi nhánh:
16 Alexandre de Rhodes - Q. I - TP Hồ Chí Minh. ĐT: (08) 38234806

In 1.000 cuốn khổ 15,5x23,2cm tại Nhà in Hội LHPN Việt Nam, Phú Thị, Gia Lâm, Hà Nội. Giấy xác nhận KHXB số: 917-2013/CXB/31-64/PN ký ngày 16/7/2013. Giấy QĐXB số: 374/QĐ-PN. In xong và nộp lưu chiểu quý IV năm 2013.